Everglades Wildguide

by Jean Craighead George
Illustrations by Betty Fraser

The Natural History of
Everglades National
Park, Florida

Produced by the
Division of Publications
National Park Service

U.S. Department of the Interior
Washington, D.C. 1988

WITHDRAWN

About This Book
Here is the story of the plants and animals of the
Everglades, this country's subtropical kingdom. Plants
and animals found nowhere else in the 50 states are
found here in abundance, though in an increasingly
perilous state. In this handbook, first published in 1972,
author and researcher Jean Craighead George brings
to the telling of this story long years of study and
understanding. Checklists and glossaries at the back
buttress her account of the natural history of this
national park.

National Park Handbooks, compact introductions to the
great natural and historic places administered by the
National Park Service, are published to support the
National Park Service's management programs at the
parks and to promote understanding and enjoyment of
the parks. Each is intended to be informative reading
and a useful guide before, during, and after a park visit.
More than 100 titles are in print. This is Handbook
143. You may purchase the handbooks through the
mail by writing to Superintendent of Documents, U.S.
Government Printing Office, Washington, DC 20402.

Library of Congress card number: 73-600077
ISBN 0-912627-29-8

PREFACE

Before the 20th century, the shimmering waters of the everglades crept silently down the tip of Florida under warm subtropical skies. In a vast, shallow sheet this lazy river idled through tall grasses and shadowy forests, easing over alligator holes and under bird rookeries, finally mingling with the salty waters of Florida Bay and the Gulf of Mexico in the mangrove swamps. From source to sea, all across the shallow breadth of this watery landscape, life was abundant.

Everglades National Park is a remnant of this Eden where birds, mammals, reptiles, and orchids find sanctuary. Sunshine sparkles on sloughs teeming with fish, and on marshes where wildflowers bloom the year around; it shines on tree islands where birds roost and deer bed down. In this semitropical garden of plant-and-animal communities, every breeze-touched glade, every cluster of trees is a separate world in which are tucked yet smaller worlds of such complexity that even ecologists have not learned all their intricate relationships.

What has changed is the water. The original sheetflow into the park has been channelized and diverted to provide flood control and water for South Florida's burgeoning population. The water that does arrive may be polluted by agricultural and urban runoff. And the water may not arrive in harmony with natural rhythms, or in places where it historically flowed. Today, the park is on life support.

In 2000, the Federal Government passed legislation to restore parts of the everglades ecosystem. The project, called the Comprehensive Everglades Restoration Plan, will take 36 years to complete, and supports all of the south Florida national parks and preserves. This book, originally published in 1978, will help you see how the many pieces of this ecological puzzle fit together to form a complex, ever-changing, closely woven web of plants, animals, rock, soil, sun, water, and air.

AMERICA'S
SUBTROPICAL WONDERLAND

Everglades may not be our largest national park
(that honor belongs to Wrangell-St. Elias in
Alaska), but it is certainly the wettest. During and
after the rainy season, when not only the mangrove
swamp but also the sawgrass prairie is under water,
most of the park abounds in fish and other water
life, and even the white-tailed deer leads a semi-
aquatic existence.

Despite the fact that it is low, flat, and largely under
water, Everglades is a park of many environments:
shallow, key-dotted Florida Bay; the coastal
prairie; the vast mangrove forest and its mysterious
waterways; cypress swamps; the true everglades
—an extensive freshwater marsh dotted with tree
islands and occasional ponds; and the driest zone,
the pine-and-hammock rockland.

The watery expanse we call "everglades," from
which the park gets its name, lies only partly within
the park boundaries. Originally this river flowed,
unobstructed though very slowly, southward from
Lake Okeechobee more than 100 miles to Florida
Bay. It is hardly recognizable as a river, for it is
50 miles wide and averages only about 6 inches
deep, and it creeps rather than flows. Its source,
the area around Lake Okeechobee, is only about
15 feet above sea level, and the riverbed slopes
southward only 2 or 3 inches to the mile.

As you can see by the maps on pages 2 and 3,
the works of man have greatly altered the drainage patterns and the natural values of south
Florida, and you can imagine how this has affected the supply of water—the park's lifeblood.

The park's array of plants and animals is a blend of
tropical species, most of which made their way
across the water from the Caribbean islands, and
species from the Temperate Zone, which embraces
all of Florida. All of these inhabitants exist here

1

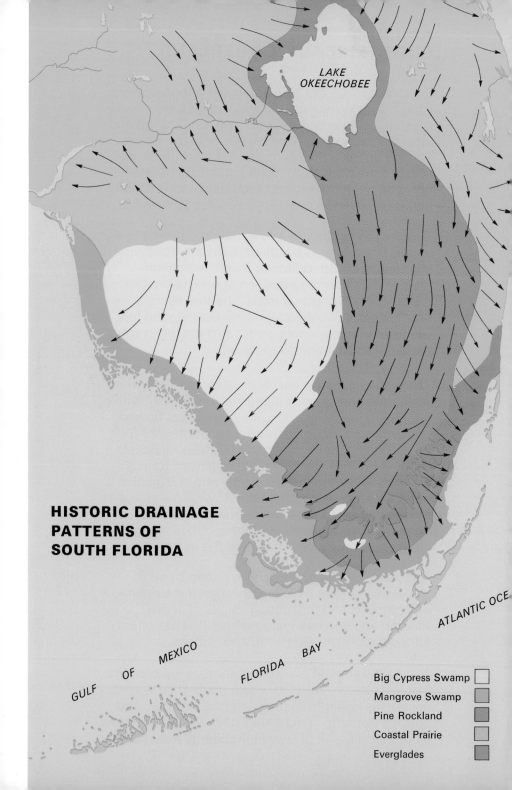

LAKE
OKEECHOBEE

**HISTORIC DRAINAGE
PATTERNS OF
SOUTH FLORIDA**

ATLANTIC OCE

GULF OF MEXICO

FLORIDA BAY

Big Cypress Swamp

Mangrove Swamp

Pine Rockland

Coastal Prairie

Everglades

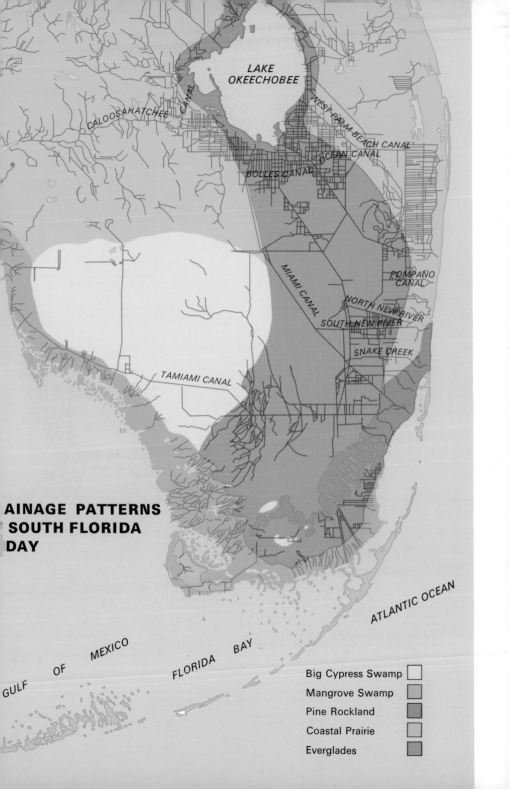

LAKE
OKEECHOBEE

CALOOSAHATCHEE CANAL

WEST PALM BEACH CANAL

OCEAN CANAL

BOLLES CANAL

MIAMI CANAL

POMPANO
CANAL

NORTH NEW RIVER

SOUTH NEW RIVER

SNAKE CREEK

TAMIAMI CANAL

AINAGE PATTERNS
SOUTH FLORIDA
DAY

ATLANTIC OCEAN

GULF   OF   MEXICO

FLORIDA   BAY

Big Cypress Swamp

Mangrove Swamp

Pine Rockland

Coastal Prairie

Everglades

PLANT COMMUNITIES
OF EVERGLADES NATIONAL PARK

The horizontal distance represented on this diagram, from the Pineland to Florida Bay, is 15 miles. With a greatly exaggerated vertical scale, the difference between the greatest elevation of the pine ridge and the bottom of the Florida Bay marl bed is only 14 feet.

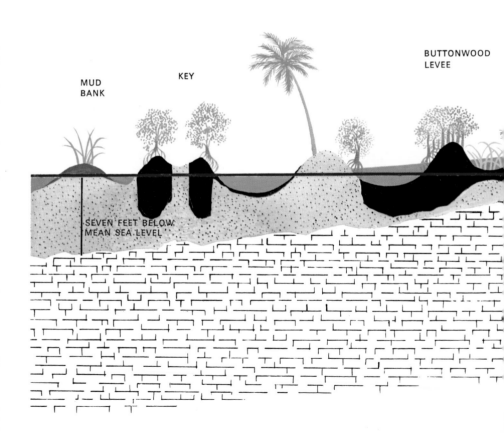

FLORIDA BAY

(SALT WATER)

COASTAL PRAIRIE

MANGROVE SWAMP

(BRACKISH)

BUTTONWOOD LEVEE

KEY

MUD BANK

SEVEN FEET BELOW MEAN SEA LEVEL

PEAT   MUD

MARL   OÖLITIC LIMESTONE

TREE-ISLAND GLADES

(FRESH WATER)

PINE AND
HAMMOCK RIDGE

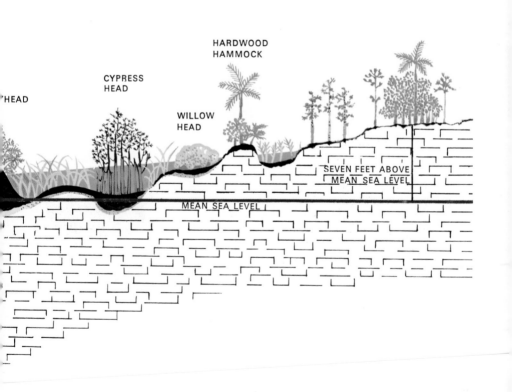

HARDWOOD
HAMMOCK

CYPRESS
HEAD

HEAD

WILLOW
HEAD

SEVEN FEET ABOVE
MEAN SEA LEVEL

MEAN SEA LEVEL

through adaptation to the region's peculiar cycles of flood, drought, and fire and by virtue of subtle variations in temperature, altitude, and soil.

Underlying the entire park is porous limestone (*see* glossary), which was deposited ages ago in warm seas that covered the southern part of today's Florida peninsula. Over this limestone only a thin mantle of marl and peat provides soil for rooting plants.

Some of the park's ecosystems (*see* glossary) are extremely complex. For example, a single jungle hammock of a dozen acres may contain, along with giant live oaks and other plants from the Temperate Zone, many kinds of tropical hardwood trees; a profusion of vines, mosses, ferns, orchids, and air plants; and a great variety of vertebrate and invertebrate animals, from tree snails to the white-tailed deer.

Pine Rockland

Entering the park from the northeast, you are on a road traversing the pineland-and-hammock "ridge." This elevated part of the South Florida limestone bedrock, which at the park entrance is about 6 feet above sea level, is the driest zone in the park. Pine trees, which will grow only on ground that remains above water most of the year, thrive on this rockland.

There is another condition essential to the survival of the pine forest in this region—fire. We usually think of fire as the enemy of forest vegetation; but that is not true here. The pines that grow in this part of Florida have a natural resistance to fire. Their thick, corky bark insulates their trunks from the flames. And strangely enough the fire actually seems to help with pine reproduction; it destroys competing vegetation and exposes the mineral soil seedlings need. If there has been a good cone crop, you will find an abundant growth of pine seedlings after a fire in the pinelands.

What would happen if the pinelands were protected from fire? Examine a pine forest where there have been no recent fires. You will note that there are many small hardwood (broadleaved) trees growing in the shade of the pines. These hardwoods would eventually shade out the light-demanding pine seedlings, and take over as the old pines died off. But under normal conditions, lightning-caused fires sweep at fairly frequent intervals through the pineland. Since the hardwoods have little resistance to fire, they are pruned back.

Before this century, fires burned vast areas. The only barriers were natural waterways—sloughs, lakes and ponds, and estuaries—which retained some water during the rainless season when the rest of the glades and pinelands dried up. Old-timers say that sometimes a fire would travel all the way from Lake Okeechobee to the coastal prairie of Cape Sable (*see* page 2). In the pine forest, any

PINE AND HAMMOCK RIDGE

(elevation: 3 to 7 feet above sea level)

HUMUS

OÖLITIC LIMESTONE

SAWGRASS
GLADES

PINELAND

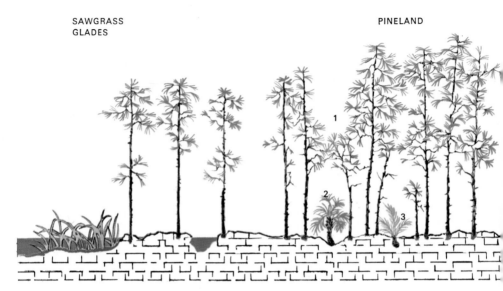

area bypassed by these fires for a lengthy period
developed into a junglelike island of hardwoods.
We call such stands "hammocks," whether they
develop in the pine forest or in the open glades.
On the limestone ridge, the hammocks support a
community of plants and animals strikingly different
from the surrounding pine forests.

With the opening up of south Florida for farming
and industry, man's works—particularly roads and
canals—soon crisscrossed the region, forming
barriers to the spread of the fires. Suppression of
fire by farmers, lumbermen, and park managers also
lessened their effect. Thus the hardwoods, which
previously had been held back by fire, tended to
replace the pines. And although the park was
established to preserve a patch of primitive
subtropical America as it was in earlier centuries,
the landscape began to change.

1 SOUTH FLORIDA SLASH PINE
2 SAW-PALMETTO
3 COONTIE
4 SAW-PALMETTO AFTER FIRE

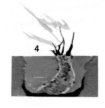

HARDWOOD
HAMMOCK

PINELAND

Continued protection of the park from fire would in
time eliminate the pineland—a plant community
that has little chance to survive elsewhere. So, in
Everglades National Park, Smokey Bear must take
a back seat : park rangers deliberately set fires to
help nature maintain the natural scene. Thus, as
you drive down the road to Flamingo, do not be
shocked to discover park rangers burning the
vegetation. The fires are controlled, of course, and
the existing hammocks are not destroyed.

When you visit the park take a close look at the
pinelands community. Notice, as you walk on the
manmade trail through the pine forest, that the
ground on either side of you is extremely rough.
The limestone bedrock is visible everywhere ; what
soil there is has accumulated in the pits and potholes
that riddle the bedrock. The trees, shrubs, grasses,
and other plants are rooted in these pockets of soil.

The limestone looks rather hazardous to walk on —and it is. You must be careful not to break through a thin shell of rock covering a cavity. This pitted, honeycombed condition is due to the fact that the limestone is easily dissolved by acids. Decaying pine needles, palmetto leaves, and other dead plant materials produce weak acids that continually eat away at the rock.

If a fire has passed through the pineland recently, you may notice that while most of the low-growing plants have been killed, some, such as the saw-palmetto, are sending up new green shoots. The thick, stubby stem of the palmetto lies in a pothole, with its roots in the soil that has accumulated there; even in the dry season the pocket in the limestone remains damp, for water is never very far below the surface in this region. When fire kills the top of the plant, the stem and roots survive, and the palmetto, like the pine, remains a part of the plant community.

A number of other plants of the south Florida pine-lands have adapted to the conditions of periodic burning. Coontie (a cycad, from the underground stems of which the Indians made flour) and moon vine (a morningglory) are among many you will see surviving pineland fires severe enough to result in the death or stunting of the hardwood seedlings and saplings.

Sometimes we forget that fire—like water, wind, and sunlight—is a natural force that operates with the others to influence the evolution of plants as well as to shape the landscape.

The pineland, like other plant communities, has its own community of animals. Some of its residents, such as the cotton mouse, opossum, and raccoon, are found in other communities of the park, too.

Some of the pineland animals, however—pine warbler, reef gecko, and five-lined skink, for example —are particularly adapted to this environment. These lovers of sunlight are dependent, like the pine forest, on the occasional natural or manmade fires that hold back the hardwood trees.

The pine rockland is quite different from the other plant-and-animal communities you will see as you drive through the park : it is the only ecosystem you can explore on foot in any season. Other parts of the park are largely flooded during the wet season. Elevated boardwalks have been provided in some of these areas to enable you to penetrate them a short distance from the road.

As you will see, fire plays an important role in some of the other Everglades communities, too.

Tree-island Glades

(elevation : 1 to 3 feet above sea level)

PEAT AND MARL

OÖLITIC LIMESTONE

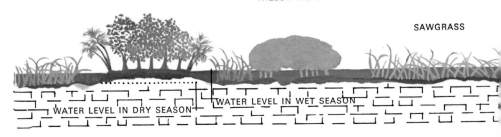

BAYHEAD

WILLOW HEAD

SAWGRASS

WATER LEVEL IN DRY SEASON

WATER LEVEL IN WET SEASON

PIG FROG
one-third life size

SQUIRREL TREEFROG

color
variation

GREEN TREEFROG
one-third life size

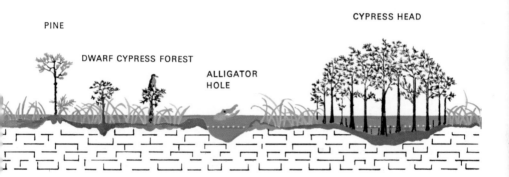

PINE

CYPRESS HEAD

DWARF CYPRESS FOREST

ALLIGATOR
HOLE

Beyond the pinelands the road, having descended
some 2 feet from the park entrance, brings you into
the true everglades—the river of grass, or, as the
Seminoles call it, Pa-Hay-Okee (grassy waters).
To the eye, the glades look like a very flat, grassy
prairie broken by scattered clumps of trees. During
the dry season (winter) it is in fact a prairie—and
sometimes burns fiercely. The dominant everglades
plant is sawgrass (actually not a grass but a sedge).
The tree islands develop in both high and low spots
of the glades terrain. In this unbelievably flat
country, small differences in elevation—measured
in inches rather than feet—cause major differences
in the plantlife : tropical hardwoods on the "mesas,"
and swamp trees in the potholes.

A spot in the glades where the limestone base is
elevated just 2 feet will be occupied by a small
13 forest of tropical hardwoods and palms—a

"hammock" much like those of the pinelands. A low spot—just a few inches below the general level of the limestone base—will remain wet even in the relatively rainless winter when the sawgrass becomes tinder dry. This sloughlike depression will support a stand of baldcypress, called a "cypress head." Other tree islands, called bayheads and willow heads, develop in many places where soil and peat accumulate.

Step from the sawgrass glades into one of these hammocks or heads; you will find yourself in another world. You cannot know the park until you have investigated these plant-and-animal communities so distinct from the surrounding marsh yet so much a part of it. As you drive through the park, look for the trails provided to give you easy access into the interior of the tree islands.

Also characteristic of the glades are the sloughs— channels where the glades water, generally a thin, seemingly motionless sheet, is deeper and has a noticeable current. The sloughs support a rich plantlife and attract a variety of animals, particularly during the dry season when the water level drops below the shallow glades bottom. Animals that live in the glades when they are under water must migrate or estivate (*see* glossary) if they are to survive the rainless months. Many migrate to the sloughs, the best known of which is Taylor Slough, where the elevated Anhinga Trail enables you to walk over the water and observe the wildlife.

Fire is an important factor in the ecology of the tree-island glades, just as it is in the pineland. Here, too, artificial barriers such as canals and roads have hindered the spread of natural fires. There is some evidence that tree islands were scattered more thinly over the sawgrass prairie a half-century ago, when a single fire might wipe out scores of them and destroy much of the bed of peat that provided a foothold for them. A bird's-eye view of the glades region today shows many tree islands that have been established in recent decades. But park rangers are now utilizing

14

controlled fires in the glades as well as in the pineland. This tends to prevent new tree islands from taking hold, and thus helps maintain the natural everglades landscape.

Driving over the glades toward Florida Bay, you come to a sign reading "Rock Reef Pass— Elevation 3 Feet." The road then traverses the so-called dwarf cypress forest. The forest is an open area of scattered, stunted baldcypress grow- ing where marl (which, unlike peat, does not burn) has accumulated in small potholes dissolved in the limestone. These marl potholes provide a foothold for the dwarf cypresses in an area that is spotted with cypress heads containing much larger trees. Many of the dwarf cypresses are more than 100 years old, while tall cypresses in the heads may be less than 50 years old. These anomalies can be attributed to varying soil depths and water levels and to the effects of fire.

Before you reach the limit of the fresh-water marsh you will come to a side road leading to Mahogany Hammock. (A good foot trail makes it easy to explore this hardwood jungle island.) Just beyond, you will notice the first red mangroves. Small and scattered in this zone, they are a signal that you are approaching a strikingly different plant-and-animal community, the mangrove swamp.

Mangrove Swamp

(elevation: sea level to 1 foot above sea level)

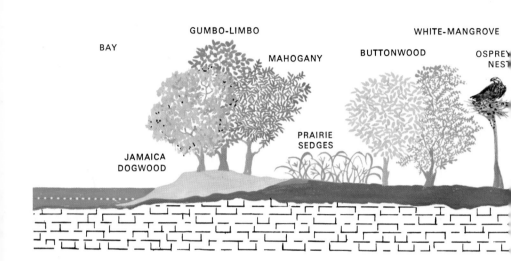

BAY

GUMBO-LIMBO

MAHOGANY

WHITE-MANGROVE

BUTTONWOOD

OSPREY NEST

PRAIRIE SEDGES

JAMAICA DOGWOOD

BONEFISH
Comes in with the tide to feed on crabs
and mollusks in shallow water

FLORIDA HORN SHELL
Lives in shallow water and
feeds upon algae
and other aquatic plants

'COON OYSTER
A small (1½") oyster
that lives attached to
the roots of mangroves

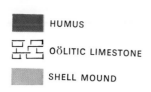

HUMUS

OÖLITIC LIMESTONE

SHELL MOUND

ESTUARY

BLACK-MANGROVE

RED MANGROVE
(very dense growth)

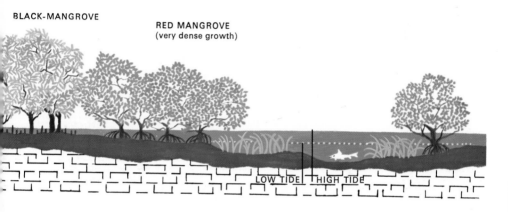

LOW TIDE | HIGH TIDE

The southward-creeping waters of the glades eventually meet and mingle with the salty waters of the tidal estuaries. In this transition zone and along the gulf and Florida Bay coasts a group of trees that are tolerant of salty conditions, called "mangroves," form a vast, watery wilderness. Impenetrable except by boat, it occupies hundreds of square miles, embracing both the shifting zone of brackish water and the saltier coastal waters.

Several kinds of trees are loosely called "mangroves." The water-tolerant red mangrove grows well out into the mudflats and is easily recognized by its arching stiltlike roots. Black-mangrove typically grows at levels covered by high tide but exposed at low tide, and it is characterized by the root projections called pneumatophores that stick up out of the mud like so many stalks of asparagus growing in the shade of the tree. White-mangrove has no peculiar root structure and grows, generally, farther from the water, behind the other trees. Sometimes all three are found in mixed stands.

This mangrove wilderness, laced by thousands of miles of estuarine channels (called "rivers" and "creeks") and broken by numerous bays and sounds, is extremely productive biologically. The brackish zone is particularly valuable as a nursery ground for shrimp. The larvae and young of these marine crustaceans and of other marine animals remain in this relatively protected environment until they are large enough to venture into the open waters beyond the mangroves.

The shrimp represent a multi-million-dollar industry, and the sports-fishing business of the area is said to exceed that by far. Both would suffer if any damage

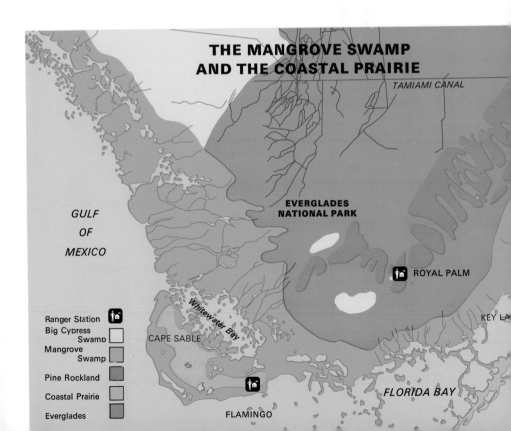

THE MANGROVE SWAMP
AND THE COASTAL PRAIRIE

TAMIAMI CANAL

EVERGLADES
NATIONAL PARK

GULF
OF
MEXICO

ROYAL PALM

Whitewater Bay

KEY LA

Ranger Station
Big Cypress
Swamp
Mangrove
Swamp
Pine Rockland
Coastal Prairie
Everglades

CAPE SABLE

FLORIDA BAY

FLAMINGO

occurred to this ecosystem. The greatest danger is the alteration in the flow of fresh waters from the glades and cypress swamps that occurs when new canals are built and land is drained for cultivation or development. The flow carries with it into the estuaries organic materials from the rich glades ecosystem; these supplement the vast quantities of organic matter derived from the decay of red mangrove leaves. Thus, a reduction in the amount of nutrient-laden fresh water flowing into the mangrove region will affect the welfare of the ecosystem, and indirectly the livelihood or recreation of many persons.

The productive zone of brackish water varies in breadth according to the flow of fresh water. In the wet summer it moves seaward as the flow of fresh water from the glades pushes the tides back. In the drier winter the bay and gulf waters move inland and the brackish zone is quite narrow. The drainage and canal-building operations in south Florida can be extremely disruptive here, since too little, or too much, fresh water flowing into the estuaries can interfere with their productivity.

Natural disasters such as hurricanes can also bring about great changes in the mangrove ecosystem. Yet biologists do not necessarily view the destruction of mangroves by hurricanes as catastrophic. The hurricanes have been occurring as long as the mangroves have grown here and are part of the complex of natural forces making the region what it is.

Fire does not seem to be a problem in the mangrove wilderness. The trees themselves are not especially fire-resistant, but it is not uncommon to see a glades fire burn to the edge of the mangroves and stop when it runs out of fine fuel.

The mangrove wilderness is a mecca for many park visitors. Sportsmen take their motorboats into the bays and rivers to challenge the fighting tarpon. Bird lovers seek the roosts and rookeries of herons and wood storks. Canoeists, the only ones able to explore the secret depths, are drawn by the spell of labyrinthine channels under arching mangrove branches. Here, in a wilderness still thwarting man's efforts at destruction, one experiences a feeling of utter isolation from the machine world.

But the relentlessly rising sea of the past 10,000 years has belittled drought, fire, hurricane, and frost as it slowly inundated this land 3 inches each hundred years. In compensation, the mangrove forest adds peat and rises with the sea. The sawgrass marshes retreat, and the mangrove ecosystem prevails essentially unchanged.

APPLE MUREX
A carnivorous mollusk that
feeds on oysters.

Florida Bay
and the Coastal Prairie

When you reach Flamingo, a former fishing village
and now a center for visitor services and accom-
modations, you will be on the shore of Florida Bay.
Here is an environment rich in variety of animal
life, where porpoises play, the American crocodile
makes its last stand, and the great white heron, once
feared doomed to extinction, holds its own. The
abundance of game fish in the bay has given it a
reputation as one of the best sport-fishing grounds
on the east coast.

The bay's approximately 100 keys (low-lying islets)
were built up by mangroves and provide foothold
for other plants hardy enough to withstand the
salty environment and the sometimes violent winds.
The keys are also a breeding ground for water
birds, ospreys, and bald eagles.

Florida Bay, larger than some of our States, is so
shallow that at low tide some of it is out of water;
its greatest depth is about 9 feet. The shallows and
mudflats attract great numbers of wading birds,
which feed upon the abundant life sheltered in the
seaweeds—a plant-and-animal community nour-
ished by nutrients carried in the waters flowing
from the glades and mangroves.

To the west beyond Flamingo is Cape Sable.
This near-island includes the finest of the
park's beaches and much of the coastal prairie
ecosystem. A fringe of coconut palms along the
beach could be the remnants of early attempts at a
plantation on the cape that did not survive the
hurricanes; or it could be the result of the sprouting
of coconuts carried by currents from Caribbean
plantations and washed up on the cape. For a
time, casuarina trees (called "Australian pines"),
which became established on Cape Sable after
Hurricane Donna, seemed to threaten the ecology
of the beach. But these invaders were mostly removed in 1971, and now appear to be under control.

21 Examine the "sand" of this beach. You will

FLORIDA BAY AND THE COASTAL PRAIRIE

(elevation: sea level to 2 feet above sea level)

1 RED MANGROVE

2 BLACK-MANGROVE

3 WHITE-MANGROVE

4 BUTTONWOOD

5 CABBAGE PALMETTO

6 HURRICANE-KILLED BLACK-MANGROVES

7 FIG

8 POISONWOOD

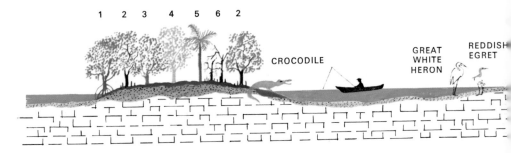

discover that it is not quartz grains—but mostly minute shell fragments.   Entire shells of the warm-water molluscs that live offshore also wash up on the beach.   There are also artifacts that speak of Indian activity in this area in past centuries, curled centers of conch shells from which the pre-Columbian Indians fashioned tools, and numerous pieces of pottery (potsherds).   Both shells and potsherds tempt the collector.   Shelling —that is, the collecting of *dead* shells, for non-commercial purposes—is permitted.   But Federal law prohibits the removal of even a fragment of pottery—for these are invaluable Indian relics, essential to continuing scientific investigation of the human history of the region.

Back from the narrow beach is a drier zone of grasses and other low-growing vegetation.   Some of the plants of this zone, such as the railroad vine,

22

MARL   HUMUS   SHELL BEACH

DUNE
(old shell beach)   MUD BEACH   OÖLITIC LIMESTONE

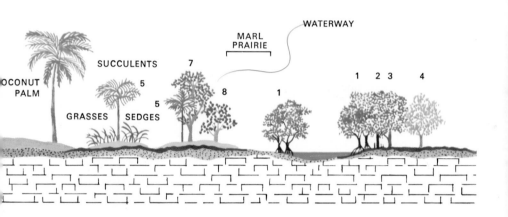

WATERWAY

MARL
PRAIRIE

SUCCULENTS   7

COCONUT
PALM   5

1 2 3   4

8   1

5

GRASSES   SEDGES

are so salt-tolerant that in places they grow almost to the water's edge. (No plant that is extremely sensitive to salty soil could survive on Cape Sable.) Beyond the grassy zone is a zone of hardwoods (buttonwood, gumbo-limbo, Jamaica dogwood), cactuses, yucca, and other plants forming a transition from beach to coastal prairie.

Birds provide much of the visual excitement of the beach community, just as they do in other parts of the park. Sandpipers, pelicans, gulls, egrets, ospreys, and bald eagles use it and the bordering waters for feeding, nesting, and resting. Mammals, notably raccoons, stalk the beach in search of food. And the big loggerhead turtle depends on it for nesting. In late spring and early summer the female loggerhead hauls herself up on the beach and digs a hole above hightide mark. There she deposits about 100 ping-pong balls—which should hatch

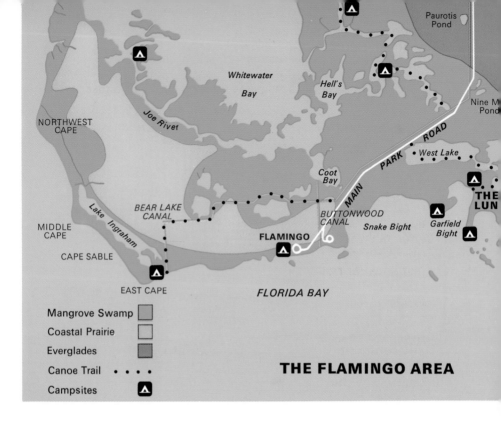

Paurotis
Pond

Whitewater
Bay

Hell's
Bay

Nine M
Pond

NORTHWEST
CAPE

Joe River

PARK ROAD

West Lake

Coot
Bay

MAIN

BEAR LAKE
CANAL

Lake Ingraham

BUTTONWOOD
CANAL

Snake Bight

Garfield
Bight

THE
LUN

MIDDLE
CAPE

FLAMINGO

CAPE SABLE

EAST CAPE

FLORIDA BAY

Mangrove Swamp

Coastal Prairie

Everglades

Canoe Trail   • • • •

Campsites

THE FLAMINGO AREA

out into baby loggerheads. Unfortunately for this marine reptile, however, most of them meet another fate. Hardly has the female turtle covered the eggs with sand and started back toward the water, than they are dug up and devoured by raccoons and other predators. These conditions created such high mortality of the turtles that the National Park Service has adopted special protective measures— removing some of the raccoons and erecting wire barriers around turtle nests. These measures have been effective, but continued surveillance is required if the loggerhead is not to disappear from Florida.

An abundance of raccoons and other predators is not the only threat to survival of the loggerhead turtle. A major factor in its decline is the serious depletion of its nesting habitat. Park visitors are prohibited from interfering with these reptiles.

24

Cape Sable beach is today virtually the only wild beach in South Florida, thanks to its inclusion in Everglades National Park. At present, visitors can reach it only by boat. But it would be foolhardy to take it for granted that the beach will remain unspoiled. Its potential as an attraction is such that someone not ecologically aware might believe that access for motorists would be an improvement. Roads, however, would bring increased pressure on the ecosystem by large numbers of visitors, and demands for further development, for lodging, meals, and other services seem always to go with automobiles. With continued protection from such encroachments, Cape Sable Beach will remain a unique wilderness resource and will not become just another recreational facility.

Merging with the beach is the coastal prairie, an ecosystem supporting red and black mangroves, grasses, and other plants tolerant of the very salty environment. Hardwood hammocks have developed here on Indian shell mounds, but the trees are stunted by the saline soils. Though there is no lack of water on the cape, much of the region appears arid because hurricane-lashed tides have deposited soils of marl and debris so salt-laden that only sparse vegetation develops.

Big Cypress Swamp

To the west of the great fresh-water marsh called
the everglades, lying almost entirely outside the
park, is an ecosystem vitally linked to the park.
Big Cypress Swamp is a vast, shallow basin that
includes practically all of Collier County. It is
commonly called "The Big Cypress"—not because
of the size of its trees, but because of its extent.
Most of the baldcypresses (which are not true
cypresses) are small trees, growing in open to
dense stands throughout the area. The swamp is
watered by about 50 inches of annual rainfall, the
runoff from which flows as a sheet and in sloughs
south and west to meet the coastal strip of
mangroves and low sand dunes.

Big Cypress is speckled with low limestone
outcrops, cut with shallow sloughs 1 to 2 feet deep,
and dotted with ponds and wet prairies. As in the
everglades, fire and water maintain the character
of the plantlife in this swampy realm of sunlight
and shadow. Also as in the everglades, a difference of a few inches in elevation creates different
communities. Tropical hardwood hammocks
grow on rocky outcrops. In the depressions arise
bayheads and clumps of pond apple, pop ash, and
willow. The larger baldcypress trees grow in
shallow sloughs, which are usually surrounded by
prairies of sawgrass and maiden cane growing on
slightly higher land. Although the several different
plant communities resemble those in the glades,
they support slightly different plants, because of the
sandy soil (there being more quartz in the limestone
under Big Cypress than in the park).

These baldcypresses, many measuring 3 to 6
feet in diameter, were heavily lumbered from 1930
to 1950. Today, few giant trees survive, but a
sizable stand exists on the Norris Tract—so named
for its conservation-minded donor—which forms
the nucleus of Corkscrew Swamp Sanctuary.
Here, protected by the National Audubon Society,
are baldcypresses 130 feet tall ; some have a girth

1 SOUTH FLORIDA SLASH PINE
2 BALDCYPRESS
3 POP ASH
4 ROYAL PALM

SANDY PEAT

FINE SAND

TAMIAMI LIMESTONE

AIR PLANT

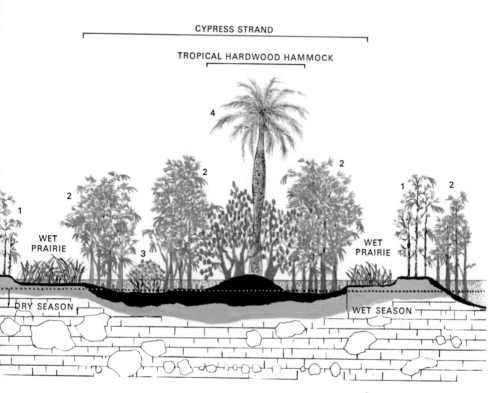

CYPRESS STRAND

TROPICAL HARDWOOD HAMMOCK

4

2

2

2

1

2

1

2

WET PRAIRIE

WET PRAIRIE

3

DRY SEASON

WET SEASON

of 25 feet!   A boardwalk more than one-half mile long enables you to enjoy the beauty of this wild preserve without getting your feet wet.

Large stands of baldcypress, called "strands," support small communities such as ponds, prairies, and tropical hammocks.   One such hammock is famous for the finest stand of royal palms remaining in south Florida.   The largest cypress strand—the Fakahatchee—extends some 23 miles north and south a few miles east of Naples.

Big Cypress Swamp is the home of wild turkey, bob-cat, deer, and an occasional Florida panther. The

27

WHITE-TAILED
DEER

OTTER

BOBCAT

fish-eating otter plays in its waterways. Most of the
birds found in the everglades also are found in the
trees and waterways of Big Cypress, because the
swamp has an abundance of food. The area is so
rich in wildlife and edible plants that the Seminole
Indians formerly lived entirely off its products.

The eastern edge of the big swamp and its importance to Everglades National Park came to
worldwide attention in 1969 when it was selected
as the site for the proposed Miami International
Jetport. According to plans, this was to be the
biggest airport in the world, covering 39 square
miles and handling 65 million passengers a year.
Millions of persons were expected to make their
home in and around the jetport. Such a threat to
the national park, into which the waters of Big
Cypress partly drain, provoked protest letters from
all over the world. Most writers objected on the
grounds that Everglades belongs to all and that a
jetport here would seal the doom of the park.
Congress acted in 1974 by establishing Big Cypress National Preserve to help protect the water
supply to Everglades National Park.

PLANT-
AND-ANIMAL COMMUNITIES

To know Everglades, you must become acquaint-
ed with some of its diverse communities. The
physical conditions determining the existence of a
particular community may seem subtle—just a few
inches difference in elevation, or an accumulation
of peat in a depression in the limestone bedrock,
for example. But often, the change in your
surroundings as you step from one community to
another is startling—for it is abrupt and complete.
In Everglades, the dividing line between two
habitats may separate an almost entirely different
association of plants and animals.

Use the trails that have been laid out to help you
see the communities. They make access easy for
you ; the rest is up to you. Be observant : notice
the stemlike root of a saw-palmetto in a damp
pothole of the pineland ; look closely at the
periphyton that plays such an important role in the
glades food chain. Note the difference in feeding
methods of wading birds ; each species has its own
niche in the habitat. Most of all, get into the
habit of thinking of each animal, each plant, as a
member of the closely woven web of life that
makes up an integrated community.

Tropical Hardwood Hammock

Generally, in south Florida, hardwood hammocks develop only in areas protected from fire, flood, and saline waters. The land must be high enough (1 to 3 feet above surrounding levels) to stand above the water that covers the glades much of the year. The roots of the trees must be out of the water and must have adequate aeration. In the park, these conditions prevail on the limestone "ridge" (elevation of which ranges from 3 to 7 feet above sea level) and some spots in the glades region. On the limestone ridge, in areas bypassed by fires for a long period, hammocks have developed. Pines grow in the surrounding areas, where repeated fires have held back the hardwoods.

The moats that tend to form around glades hammocks, as acids from decaying plant materials dissolve the limestone, hold water even during the dry season; the moats thus act as barriers protecting the hammock vegetation from glades fires.

When the white man took over southern Florida, these hammocks were luxuriant jungle islands dominated by towering tropical hardwoods and palms. Stumps and logs on the floors of some of the remaining hammocks, attesting to the enormous size of some of the earlier trees, are sad reminders of the former grandeur of the hammocks. While most of south Florida's hammocks have been destroyed, you can still see some fine ones protected in the park. At Royal Palm Hammock, near park headquarters, Gumbo Limbo Trail winds through a dim, dense forest with welcome coolness on a hot day.

Stepping into a jungle hammock from either the sunbathed glades or the open pine forest is a sudden, dramatic change. The contrast when you enter Gumbo Limbo Trail immediately after walking the Anhinga Trail is striking. While the watery world of Anhinga is dominated by a noisy profusion of wildlife, the environment of Gumbo Limbo will seem to be a mere tangle of vegetation. But the jungle hammock, too, has its community of animals—even though you may notice none but mosquitoes. Many of its denizens are nocturnal in their habits, but if you remain alert you will observe birds, invertebrates, and perhaps a lizard.

The trees that envelop you as you walk on Gumbo Limbo Trail are mostly tropical species; of the dominant trees, only the live oak (which grows as far north as Virginia) can be considered non-tropical. Under oaks and tropical bustics, poisonwood, mastics, and gumbo-limbos grow small trees such as tetrazygia, rough-leaf velvetseed, and wild coffee, a multitude of mosses and ferns, and only a few species of shade-tolerant flowering plants. Orchids and air plants burst like sun stars from limbs, trunks, and fallen logs. Twining among them all, the woody vines called lianas enhance the jungle atmosphere. Adding a final touch are the royal palms that here and there tower over the hardwood canopy—occasionally reaching 125 feet.

TREE SNAILS

There are 52 color forms of *Liguus fasciatus* found in south Florida.

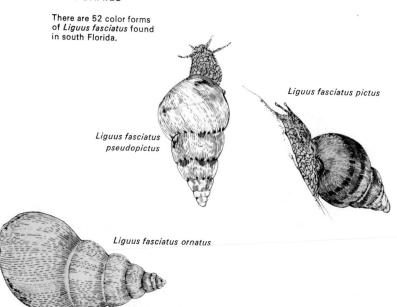

Liguus fasciatus pictus

Liguus fasciatus pseudopictus

Liguus fasciatus ornatus

TROPICAL HARDWOOD HAMMOCK

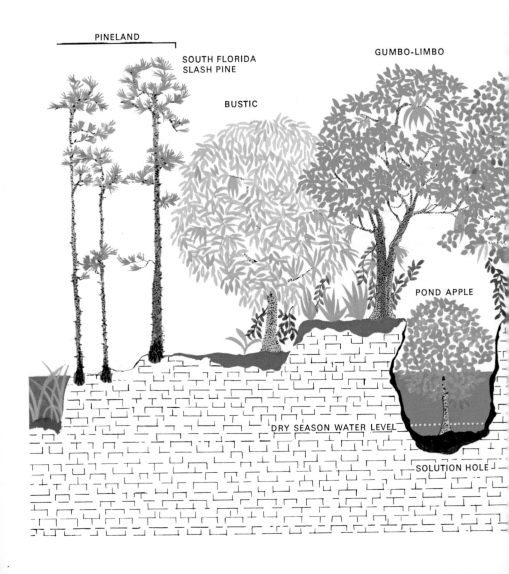

PINELAND

SOUTH FLORIDA
SLASH PINE

GUMBO-LIMBO

BUSTIC

POND APPLE

DRY SEASON WATER LEVEL

SOLUTION HOLE

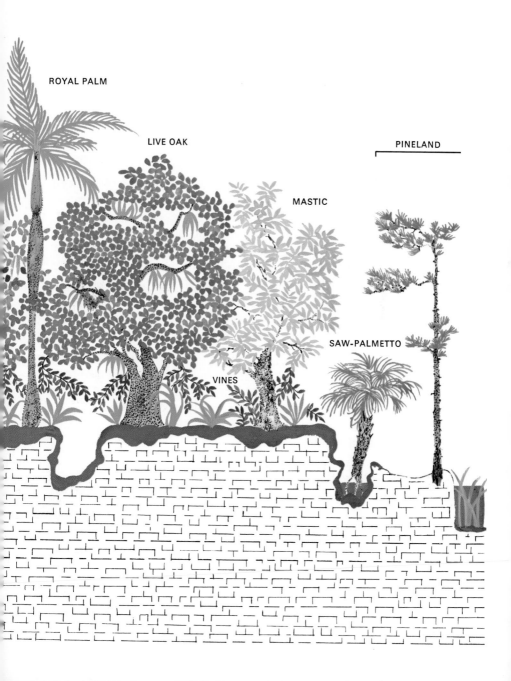

HUMUS

PEAT

OÖLITIC LIMESTONE

AIR PLANTS
(ORCHIDS, BROMELIADS)

ROYAL PALM

LIVE OAK

PINELAND

MASTIC

SAW-PALMETTO

VINES

The limestone rock that underlies the entire park is porous and soluble; consequently the floor of the hammock is pitted with solution holes dissolved by the acid from decaying vegetation. Soil and peat accumulating in the water-filled bottom of one of these holes supports a plant community of its own: perhaps a pond apple, surrounded by ferns and mosses (including some varieties that seem to be limited to this pothole environment).

A dead, decaying log on the ground may support another miniature plant community—a carpet of mosses, ferns, and other small plants that thrive in such moist situations.

Strangest of the hammock plants is the strangler fig, which first gets a foothold in the rough bark of a live oak, cabbage palm, or other tree. It then sends roots down to the ground, entwining about the host tree as it grows, and eventually killing it. On the Gumbo Limbo Trail you will see a strangler fig that grew in this manner and was enmeshed by another strangler fig—which now is threatened by a third fig that already has gained a foothold in its branches.

Best known of the glades hammocks is Mahogany Hammock. A boardwalk trail in this lush, junglelike tree island leads past the giant mahogany tree for which the hammock was named—now, because of Hurricane Donna, a dismembered giant. This fine tree island was explored only after the park was established.

An array of large and small vertebrate animals, mostly representative of the Temperate Zone, populates these tropical hardwood jungles: raccoons and opossums, many varieties of birds, snakes and lizards, tree frogs, even bobcats and the rare Florida panther, or cougar. Not surprisingly, invertebrates—including insects and snails—abound in this luxuriant plant community. The tropical influence is evident in the presence of invertebrates such as tree snails of the genus *Liguus*, known outside of Florida only in Hispaniola and Cuba.

Cypress Head

MARL

PEAT

OÖLITIC LIMESTONE

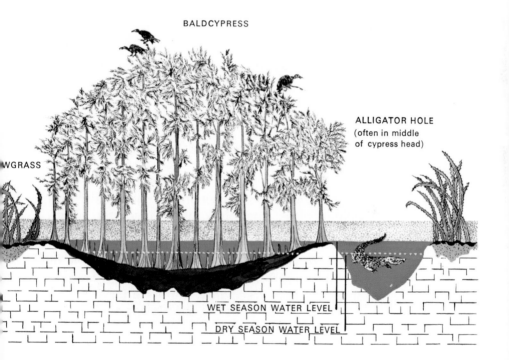

BALDCYPRESS

ALLIGATOR HOLE
(often in middle
of cypress head)

WGRASS

WET SEASON WATER LEVEL

DRY SEASON WATER LEVEL

Standing out conspicuously on the glades landscape are tall, domelike tree islands of baldcypress.   Unlike hammocks, which occupy elevations, cypress heads, or domes, occupy depressions in the limestone bedrock—areas that remain as ponds or wet places during seasons when the glades dry up.   Water-loving cypresses need only a thin accumulation of peat and soil to begin their growth in these depressions or in smaller solution holes in the limestone.

35

TURKEY VULTURE

Though most conifers retain their needles all year, baldcypresses shed their foliage in winter. The fallen needles decay, forming acids that dissolve the limestone further; thus these trees tend to enlarge their own ponds. Since the pond is deeper in the middle, and the accumulation of peat is greater there, the taller trees grow in the center of the head, with the smaller ones toward the edge. Hence the characteristic dome-shaped profile.

Usually when fire sweeps the glades, the baldcypresses, occupying low, wet spots, are not injured. But with extended drought, the water disappears and the peat may burn for months, killing all the baldcypresses.

The cypress heads sometimes serve as alligator holes, where the big reptiles and other aquatic animals are able to survive dry periods. As you drive along the park road, stop and examine these tree islands through your binoculars; they are favored haunts of many of the park's larger wading

36

birds.   Look for herons, egrets, wood storks, and white ibis, which visit these swampy habitats to feed on the abundant aquatic life.

Bald eagles find the tops of the tallest cypresses advantageous perches from which to scan the marsh.   And at night certain of the cypress heads are "buzzard roosts"—resting areas for gatherings of hundreds of turkey vultures.

Bayhead

ORCHIDS
AND BROMELIADS

MARL

PEAT

OÖLITIC
LIMESTONE

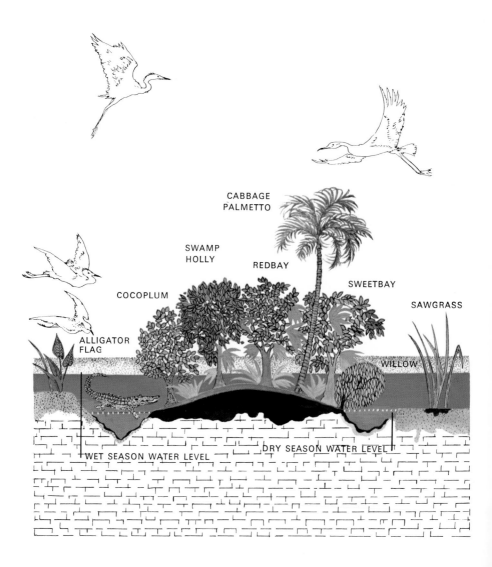

CABBAGE
PALMETTO

SWAMP
HOLLY

REDBAY

SWEETBAY

COCOPLUM

SAWGRASS

ALLIGATOR
FLAG

WILLOW

DRY SEASON WATER LEVEL

WET SEASON WATER LEVEL

Many of the tree islands in the fresh-water glades are of the type called bayhead. Growing in depressions in the limestone or from beds of peat built up on the bedrock, these plant communities contain a variety of trees, including swamp holly, redbay, sweetbay, wax myrtle, and cocoplum. Some of them, on the fringes of the brackish zone, are marked by clumps of graceful paurotis palms growing at their edges.

Like the hardwood hammocks in the pinelands, bayheads are prevented from taking over the entire glades ecosystem by the dry-season fires that sweep the region at irregular intervals. The fires do not always affect the bayheads. A moat, formed by the dissolving action of acids from decaying plant materials on the limestone, may surround the tree island, providing some protection from fire. Wildlife concentrates in these moats during the dry season. Birds congregate here to harvest the fish, snails, and other aquatic life—and occasionally themselves fall prey to lurking alligators.

Willow Head

Willows pioneer new territories and create an environment that enables other plants to gain a foothold. Their windblown seeds usually root in sunny land opened by fire and agriculture. Since these trees require a great quantity of water, the solution holes in the glades are favorable sites. Seedlings grow, leaves fall, and stems and twigs die and drop—contributing to the formation of peat. When this builds up close to or above the surface of the water, it provides a habitat for other trees such as sweet bay and cocoplum; with enough of these the willow head changes character and becomes a bayhead.

Years ago, when alligators were plentiful, they weeded the willow-bordered solution holes, keeping them open. Consequently, the willow heads were typically donut-shaped. Today, however, alligators are scarce and many of the willow heads have no 'gators. The solution holes fill with muck and peat; relatively tall willows rise out of the deep, peat-filled centers, with increasingly smaller ones toward the less fertile edges, and the willow heads take on the characteristic dome-shaped profile but not nearly the height of the cypress domes. They have a clumpy, brushy appearance, seeming to grow right out of the marsh without trunks.

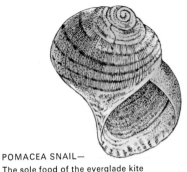

POMACEA SNAIL—
The sole food of the everglade kite

EVERGLADE KITE

MARL

PEAT

OÖLITIC LIMESTONE

Willow heads with alligator holes typically have a doughnut shape—the gator hole representing the hole in the
doughnut.

COASTAL PLAIN WILLOW

CATTAIL

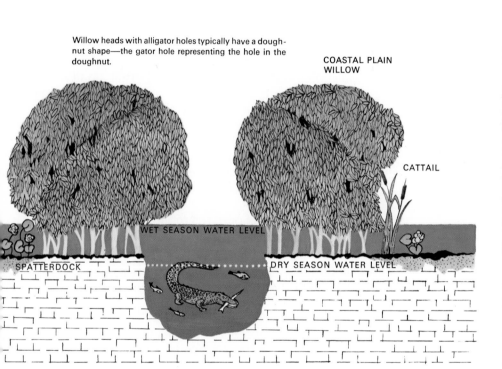

WET SEASON WATER LEVEL

SPATTERDOCK

DRY SEASON WATER LEVEL

Willow heads that do have alligator holes have a
seasonal concentration of aquatic animals and the
birds and mammals that prey upon them.   They
rarely support orchids or bromeliads, for the bark
of the southern willow is too smooth to provide
anchorage for the seedlings of these plants.

During drought periods willow heads, like bayheads,
are vulnerable to the fires that sometimes burn
over the glades.

41

Web of Life in the Marsh

Around the stems and other underwater parts of the glades plants are cylindrical masses of yellowish-green *periphyton*. So incredibly abundant are these masses of living material that in late summer the water appears as though clogged with mossy-looking sausages and floating pancakes. Largely algae, but containing perhaps 100 different organisms, the periphyton supports a complex web of glades life. It is the beginning of many food chains in the fresh-water marsh. The larvae of mosquitoes and other invertebrates, larval frogs (tadpoles) and salamanders, and other small, free-swimming creatures feed upon the tiny plants and minute animals living in the masses of periphyton. These periphyton feeders are in turn fed upon by small fish, frogs, and other vertebrates, which are food for big fish, birds, mammals, and reptiles; most of these larger creatures are preyed upon by the alligator.

The periphyton is perhaps most important for its role in maintaining the physical environment of the marsh. The water flowing over the limestone of the glades is hard with calcium. The algae remove this calcium and convert it to marl (*see* glossary), which precipitates to the bottom. Sawgrass is rooted in this marl; accumulated dead sawgrass forms peat; other marsh plants, including willows and the trees of the bayheads, spring up from the peat. Acid from the peat and from decaying plant matter of the tree islands dissolves some of the marl and underlying bedrock—and the cycle is complete.

Every plant, every animal, every physical element is involved in this web of life—as soil builder, predator, plant-eater, scavenger, agent of decay, or converter of energy and raw materials into food. Damage to or removal of any of these components —pollution of the water, lowering of the water table, elimination of a predator, or any interference in the energy cycle—could destroy the glades as we know them.

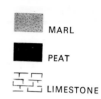

MARL

PEAT

LIMESTONE

PERIPHYTON (ALGAE
AND ONE-CELLED ANIMALS)

DEAD LEAVES AND STEMS

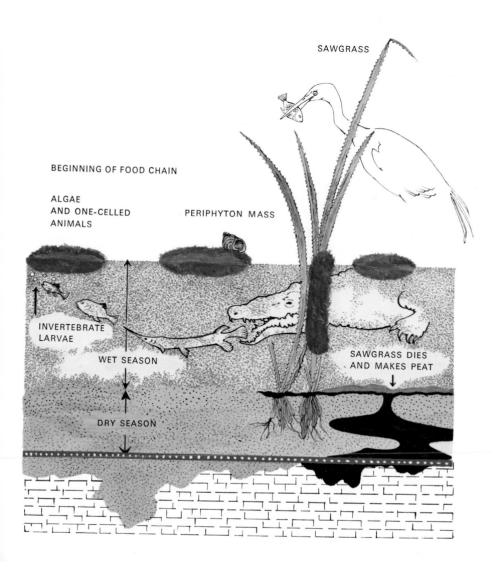

SAWGRASS

BEGINNING OF FOOD CHAIN

ALGAE
AND ONE-CELLED
ANIMALS

PERIPHYTON MASS

INVERTEBRATE
LARVAE

WET SEASON

DRY SEASON

SAWGRASS DIES
AND MAKES PEAT

Every other plant-and-animal community in the park—hammock, mangrove swamp, pineland, etc.—is an association of large and small organisms sharing a physical environment. It is impossible to understand either the park as a whole or the life of a single creature without being aware of these interrelationships.

Alligator Hole in the Glades

Out in the sunny glades the broad leaves of the
alligator flag mark the location of an alligator hole.
This is the most incredible ecosystem of all the
worlds within the world of the park; for in a sense
the alligator is the keeper of the everglades.

With feet and snout these reptiles clear out the
vegetation and muck from the larger holes in the
limestone.   In the dry season, when the floor of the
glades checks in the sun, these holes are oases.
Then large numbers of fish, turtles, snails, and
other fresh-water animals take refuge in the holes,
moving right in with the alligators.   Enough of
these water-dependent creatures thus survive the
drought to repopulate the glades when the rains
return.   Birds and mammals join the migration
of the everglades animal kingdom to the alligator
holes, feed upon the concentrated life in them—and
in turn occasionally become food for their alligator
hosts.

Lily pads float on the surface.   Around the edges
arrowleaf, cattails, and other emergent plants grow.
Behind them on higher muckland, much of which
is created by the alligators as they pile up plant
debris, stand ferns, wildflowers, and swamp trees.
Algae thrive in the water.   The rooted water plants
might become so dense as to hinder the movement

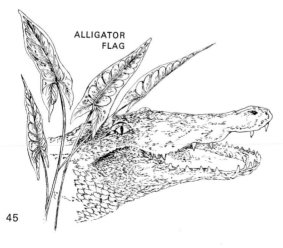

ALLIGATOR
FLAG

and growth of the fish, were it not for the weeding activities of the alligators. With the old reptiles keeping the pool open, the fish thrive, and alligator and guests live well.

Plants piled beside the hole by the alligator decay and form soil with mud and marl. Ferns, wild-flowers, and tree seedlings take root, and eventually the alligator hole may be the center of a tree island.

So, it's easy to see how important the alligator is to the ecology of the park. Unfortunately for this rep-tile, many people in the past believed only in the value of its hide. Hunting for alligators became profitable in the mid-1880s and continued until the 1960s. In 1961 Florida prohibited all hunting of alligators, but poaching continued to take its toll. Finally, the Fed-eral Endangered Species Act of 1969 protected the alligator by eliminating all hunting and trafficking in hides.

As a result of complete protection, the alligator has increased greatly in number. They are no longer an endangered species in Florida, and they can easily be found in gator holes and sloughs. Today alligators are eagerly sought by visitors to Everglades National Park who are anxious to see and photograph this unique creature. Once again, the alligator is the keeper of the everglades.

ACTUAL SIZE AT HATCHING
(8" to 10")

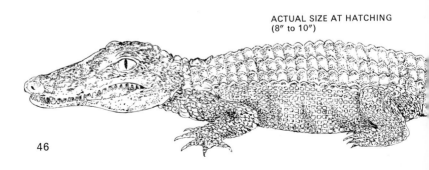

46

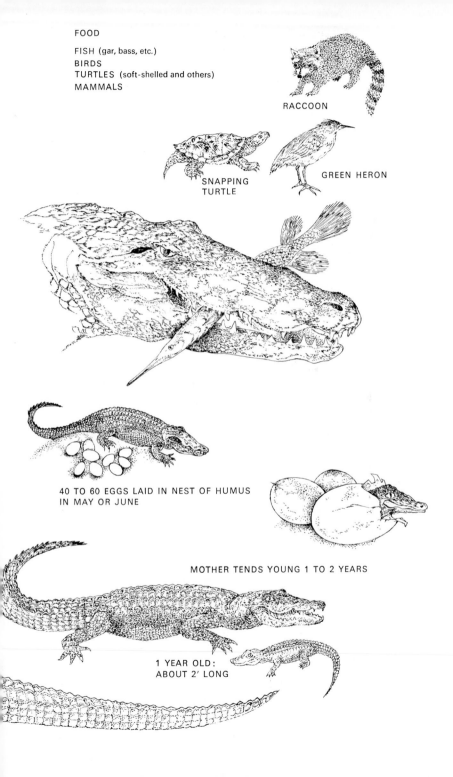

FOOD

FISH (gar, bass, etc.)
BIRDS
TURTLES (soft-shelled and others)
MAMMALS

RACCOON

SNAPPING
TURTLE

GREEN HERON

40 TO 60 EGGS LAID IN NEST OF HUMUS
IN MAY OR JUNE

MOTHER TENDS YOUNG 1 TO 2 YEARS

1 YEAR OLD:
ABOUT 2' LONG

ALLIGATOR HOLE IN THE GLADES

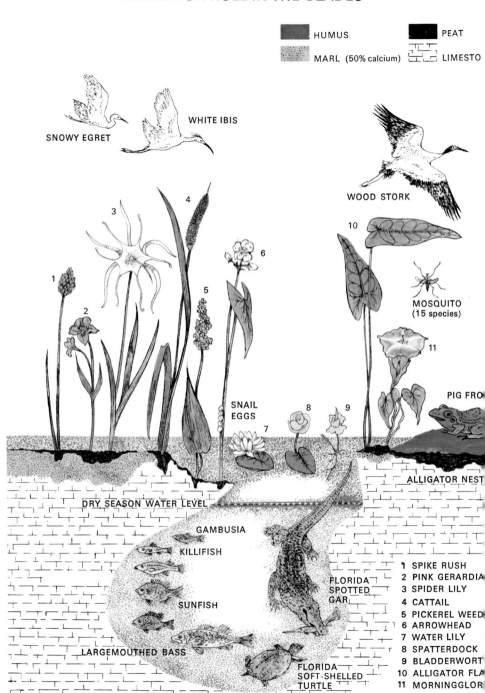

HUMUS

PEAT

MARL (50% calcium)

LIMESTO

SNOWY EGRET

WHITE IBIS

WOOD STORK

MOSQUITO
(15 species)

PIG FRO

SNAIL
EGGS

ALLIGATOR NEST

DRY SEASON WATER LEVEL

GAMBUSIA

KILLIFISH

FLORIDA
SPOTTED
GAR

SUNFISH

LARGEMOUTHED BASS

FLORIDA
SOFT-SHELLED
TURTLE

1 SPIKE RUSH
2 PINK GERARDIA
3 SPIDER LILY
4 CATTAIL
5 PICKEREL WEED
6 ARROWHEAD
7 WATER LILY
8 SPATTERDOCK
9 BLADDERWORT
10 ALLIGATOR FLA
11 MORNINGGLOR

DISCOVERING EVERGLADES
PLANTS AND ANIMALS

Everglades National Park, with its array of plant communities—ranging from the pines and palmettos rooted in the pitted limestone bedrock of the park's dry uplands, through the periphyton-based marsh community and the brackish mangrove swamp, to the highly saline waters of Florida Bay—is an amateur botanist's paradise. Many of the park's plants are found nowhere else in the United States. Only here at the southern tip of the Florida peninsula do tropical trees and orchids mingle with oaks and pines.

This book is not intended to be a manual for identification of the Everglades plants. You will need to arm yourself with appropriate field guides to ferns, orchids, aquatic plants, trees, or whatever your special interest may be. The reading list in the appendix suggests a few.

While the park is a mecca for students of plantlife, you must keep one thing in mind : your collecting will be limited to photographs (and, if you're an artist, drawings). *No specimens may be removed or disturbed*. Fortunately, with today's versatile cameras and high-quality color films you can take home a complete and accurate record of your plant discoveries.

Much of our present knowledge of Everglades plantlife has been garnered by amateurs. Much more needs to be accumulated before an environmental management program for the park can be perfected, and serious students of botany are invited to make their data available to the park staff.

As for wild animals, one hardly needs to look for them in this park ! Most visitors come here, at least partly, for that reason. And even those not seeking wildlife should be alert to avoid stepping on or running down the slower or less wary creatures. But animal watching is a great pastime, and it pays

49

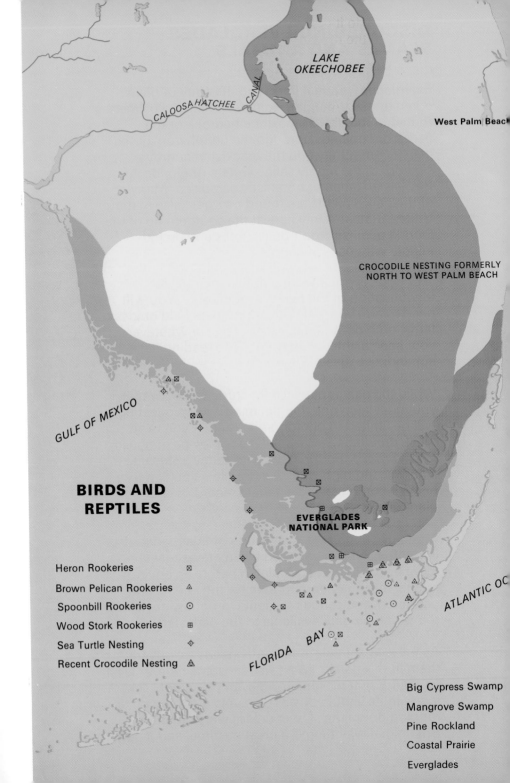

LAKE
OKEECHOBEE

CALOOSAHATCHEE CANAL

West Palm Beac

CROCODILE NESTING FORMERLY
NORTH TO WEST PALM BEACH

GULF OF MEXICO

BIRDS AND
REPTILES

EVERGLADES
NATIONAL PARK

ATLANTIC OC

FLORIDA BAY

Heron Rookeries ⊠
Brown Pelican Rookeries △
Spoonbill Rookeries ⊙
Wood Stork Rookeries ⊞
Sea Turtle Nesting ◇
Recent Crocodile Nesting △

Big Cypress Swamp
Mangrove Swamp
Pine Rockland
Coastal Prairie
Everglades

to learn to do it right.   A few suggestions may help you make the most of your experience in Everglades.

A notebook in which to record your observations will help you discover that this park is not just a landscape of grass, water, and trees where a lot of animals happen to live—but a complex, subtropical world of plant-and-animal communities, each distinct and yet dependent upon the others.   To gain real understanding of this world you will need certain skills and some good habits.   Ability to identify what you see—with the help of good field guides (*see* reading list) and quite a bit of prac-tice—will make things easier and much more enjoyable.

Knowing where to look for the animals helps; this book and the field guides are useful for this. You'll find that some species are seen only in certain parts of the park, while others roam far and wide. Don't look for the crocodile in the fresh-water glades—nor for the round-tailed muskrat in the mangroves.   On the other hand, don't be surprised to see the raccoon or its tracks in almost any part of the park.

Keep in mind that all species in the national parks are protected by law.   Most wild animals are harmless as long as they are not molested.   If you encounter an animal you aren't sure about, sim-ply keep out of its way; don't try to harm it or drive it off.   Always remember that each animal is part of the Everglades community; you cannot disturb it without affecting everything else.

Air Plants

Long before you have learned to distinguish the major plant communities, you will be aware of the air plants—or epiphytes—that grow so profusely in Everglades. Epiphytes are non-parasitic plants that grow on other plants, getting their nourishment from the air. Best known is Spanish moss, which festoons the trees of the coastal South from Virginia to Texas; this plant is used by the swallow-tailed kite in constructing its beautiful nest. Despite its name, Spanish moss is actually a member of the pineapple family—the bromeliads. Bromeliads are the most conspicuous of the park's air plants. The epiphytic orchids, though less common, are celebrated for their beauty; their fame, unfortunately, has led to their widespread destruction. There are also epiphytic ferns, trees, and vines; and one cactus, the mistletoe cactus, has taken to the air.

Air plants are highly specialized for making a living under crowded conditions; there are more than 2,000 species of plants competing for sun and water in southern Florida. The epiphytes have adapted to the problem of space by growing on other plants. Their roots, although they absorb some water and minerals, are primarily anchors. Living in an atmosphere that fluctuates between drought and humidity, they have evolved several water-conserving tricks. Some have a reduced number of leaves; others have tough skins that resist loss of water through transpiration; still others have thick stems, called pseudobulbs, that store moisture. The bromeliads are particularly ingenious: many have leaves shaped in such a way that they hold rainwater in vaselike reservoirs at their bases. Mosquitoes and tree frogs breed in these tiny reservoirs, and in dry periods many aboreal animals seek the dew that collects here.

Most of the orchids and bromeliads grow in the dimly lit tropical hardwood hammocks and cypress sloughs. A few species, however, having adapted to the sunlight, live on dwarf mangroves and the

STIFF-LEAVED WILDPINE

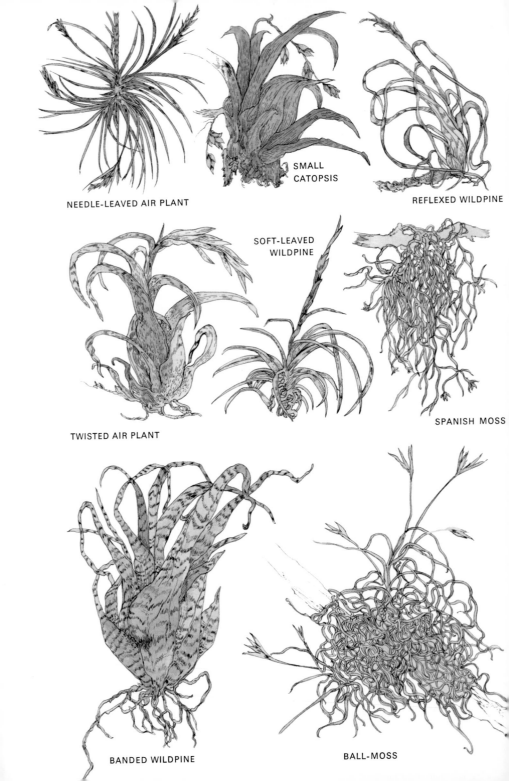

NEEDLE-LEAVED AIR PLANT

SMALL CATOPSIS

REFLEXED WILDPINE

SOFT-LEAVED WILDPINE

TWISTED AIR PLANT

SPANISH MOSS

BANDED WILDPINE

BALL-MOSS

scattered buttonwoods, pond apples, willows, and cocoplums of the glades. The butterfly and cowhorn orchids are sun lovers, as are the twisted, banded, and stiff-leaved bromeliads. All have adapted to the sun with dew-condensing mechanisms or vases at the bottom of the clustered leaves.

One tree, the strangler fig, starts as an epiphytic seedling on the branches of other trees. Eventually, however, it drops long aerial roots directly to the ground or entwines them about the trunk of the host tree—which in time dies, leaving a large fig tree in its place.

Of all Everglades plants, the epiphytic orchids are most fascinating to man—a fact which largely explains their decline. Of some 50,000 species around the world (the orchids being one of the largest of plant families), the park has only a few. Fire, loss of habitat due to agriculture and construction, and poaching by both commercial and amateur collectors have brought about the extermination of some and have made others exceedingly rare. Some are rare because of special life requirements. For example, a few must live in association with a certain fungus that coats their roots and provides specific nutrients.

The largest orchid in the park is the cowhorn, some specimens of which weigh as much as 75 pounds. Unfortunately, this orchid has been a popular item for orchid growers and collectors and is becoming rare in Florida. Poachers have practically eliminated it from the park. In the late 1960s Boy Scout friends of Everglades salvaged many orchids from hammocks about to be bulldozed for the jetport. By laboriously tying them to trees in the park, they assured the survival of the plants.

The night-blooming epidendrum is perhaps the most beautiful of the park's orchids. It is widespread and fairly common in Everglades, occurring in all ecosystems. Flowering throughout the year, it bears its white, spiderlike blossoms, 2 inches across, one at a time. It is especially fragrant at night—hence its name.

SHOWY ORCHIDS OF THE HAMMOCKS AND TREE ISLANDS

BROWN
EPIDENDRUM

NIGHT BLOOMING
EPIDENDRUM

DOLLAR ORCHID

SPREAD-EAGLE
ORCHID

BUTTERFLY ORCHID

FLORIDA
ONCIDIUM

MULE-EAR
ORCHID

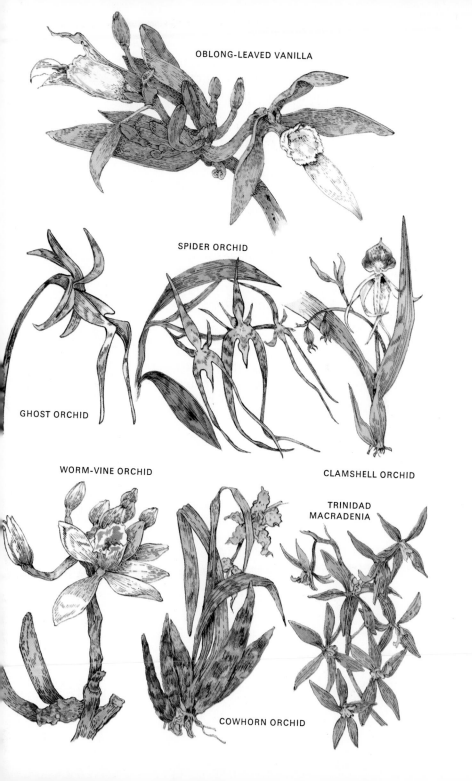

OBLONG-LEAVED VANILLA

SPIDER ORCHID

GHOST ORCHID

WORM-VINE ORCHID

CLAMSHELL ORCHID

TRINIDAD
MACRADENIA

COWHORN ORCHID

Epiphytic orchids have the smallest seeds of any flowering plants. Dustlike, they travel far and wide on the air; it is believed that over eons all species of Florida orchids arrived on the wind from South America and the West Indies.

The giant wildpine is a spectacular bromeliad that grows on the sturdy limbs of buttonwoods, spreading to 48 inches and developing a flower stalk 6 feet long.

Of the approximately 20 species of epiphytic ferns in the park, the most common is the curious resurrection fern. Sometimes called the poor man's barometer, it has leaves that in dry weather curl under and turn brown but with the coming of rain quickly unfold and turn bright green, making instant gardens of the logs, limbs, and branches on which they grow.

Watch for the air plants (as well as the trees and other wildflowers) that have been labeled along the trails and boardwalks. You will be able to examine some of them closely—but leave them unharmed for future visitors!

Mammals

In the drowned habitats of Everglades it is not surprising to find water-bound mammals such as the porpoise; or fish-eating amphibious mammals such as the otter; or even land mammals, such as the raccoon, that characteristically feed upon aquatic life. But to see mammals that one ordinarily does not associate with water behaving as though they were born to it is another matter. The white-tailed deer is an example. It is so much a part of this watery environment that you will most likely observe it far out in the glades, feeding upon aquatic plants or bounding over the marsh. Very probably the deer you see was born on one of the tree islands, and has never been out of sight of the sawgrass river.

Many other mammals of Everglades are adapted to a semi-aquatic existence. The park's only representative of the hare-and-rabbit clan is the marsh rabbit; smaller than its close relative, the familiar cottontail of fields and woodlands, it is as comfortable in this wet world as if it had webbed feet. So don't be startled if you see a rabbit swimming here! The park's rodents include the marsh rice rat and round-tailed muskrat, also at home in a watery environment.

The playful otter, though it may travel long distances overland, is a famous water-lover. Lucky is the visitor who sees a family of these large relatives of the weasel! The otter's smaller cousin, the everglades mink, is also a denizen of the marsh and a predator in the food web; but you are not likely to see this wary animal.

Raccoons and opossums, adaptable creatures that they are, live in all the park's environments—except in the air and under water. Their diets are as wide-ranging as their habitat. The raccoon, though it has a taste for aquatic animals such as fish, frogs, and crayfish, also consumes small land vertebrates and various plant foods. The opossum eats virtually anything in the animal kingdom that it can find and

SOME IMPORTANT EVERGLADES MAMMALS

SPECIES	PINE ROCKLAND	HARDWOOD HAMMOCK
Opossum	X	X
Short-tailed Shrew		
Least Shrew		
Marsh Rabbit	X	X
Fox Squirrel		
Rice Rat		
Cotton Mouse	X	X
Hispid Cotton Rat		
Florida Water Rat		
Raccoon	X	X
Black Bear	?	?
Mink		
River Otter		
Gray Fox		[1]X
Bobcat	X	X
Florida panther		X
White-tailed Deer	X	X
Bottle-nosed Dolphin		
Manatee		

[1]In pinelands.
[2]Estuaries.

)ES	MANGROVE SWAMP	FRESHWATER SWAMPS	FLORIDA BAY and KEYS	COASTAL PRAIRIE	REMARKS
X	X	X	X	X	
		X			
		X			
X		X	X	X	
	X	?			
X		X			
X		X			
				X	
X		X			
X	X	X	X	X	Abundant
?	?	?		?	Very rare
X		X			
X		X			
X	X	X		X	
X	X	X			Rare
X		X		X	
			X		
	[2] X		X		

subdue, as well as a wide variety of plant materials.

South Florida is the last known refuge in the world for a sub-species of cougar known as the Florida panther. This large, beautiful cat is on the endangered species list. Today many groups and individuals are working to keep this predator a part of the environment. Their efforts have resulted in methods to assist panther recovery: lower speed limits and highway culverts and bridges, to mention only two. With continued assistance, the panther may remain a part of the Everglades for years to come.

Because it is much more numerous and much less secretive in its habits, the bobcat is more likely to be encountered by park visitors than is the cougar. Keep your eyes alert for this wild feline—particularly in the Flamingo area—and you may have a chance to observe it closely and at some length (even by daylight!). Such boldness and such unconcern for humans are not typical of this species, but seem to be peculiarities of the bobcats living in the park. Although bobcats are not known as water lovers, they are found in all the Everglades environments. Their apparent liking for life in the park may be due to an abundance of food and to freedom from persecution by man and his dogs. Bobcats in Everglades, if their food habits elsewhere are any guide, probably live on rodents, marsh rabbits, and birds, with possibly an occasional fawn.

In Florida Bay and the estuaries, look for the porpoise, or bottlenosed dolphin, a small member of the whale order that has endeared itself to Americans through its antics at marine aquariums and on television. Watch for it when you are on a boat trip in the park's marine environment.

Much less commonly seen, and much less familiar, is the timid and very rare manatee. It's probably the "most" animal of the park—the largest (sometimes over 15 feet long and weighing nearly 1 ton), the shyest, the strangest, and the homeliest; and it is probably also the most delicate, for a drop in water temperatures may kill it. The estuaries of

Everglades National Park are almost the northern limits of its normal range. But manatees are often found well north of the park on both coasts in cold weather, when they swim up rivers to seek the constant-temperature water discharged by electric power plants. Despite its size, the manatee is a harmless creature, being a grazer—a sort of underwater cow that is exceptionally vulnerable to motorboats because of its gentle nature and languid movement.

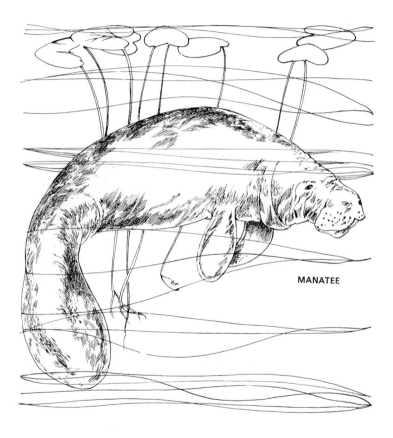

MANATEE

Birds

LONG-LEGGED WADING BIRDS
OF THE GLADES, FRESH-WATER SWAMPS,
MANGROVE SWAMPS, AND FLORIDA BAY.

BLACK-CROWNED NIGHT HERON

LOUISIANA
HERON

YELLOW-CROWNED
NIGHT HERON

GREEN HERON

From the pelican—whose mouth can hold more than its belly can—to the tiny hummingbird, the birds of Everglades National Park add beauty, amusement, excitement, and drama to the daily scene. Much more conspicuous than the park's other animals, they can be enjoyed with no special effort. But a pair of binoculars and a field guide will make bird watching a more rewarding pastime for you.

Many of the park's birds are large and colorful, and so tolerant of man's presence that you can observe them closely without the aid of binoculars. The Anhinga Trail and other sites on or near the main park road provide ready access to activity by herons and egrets, cormorants, gallinules, and other species that feed upon the fish, frogs, and lesser life of the waters.

The anhinga, after whom the park's most popular trail is named, is a favorite with visitors. It is also called water-turkey, probably because of its large size and long, white-tipped tail feathers. A third name, snake bird, derives from the anhinga's habit of swimming almost totally submerged with its long, snaky neck above the surface. The anhinga is a skilled fisherman, seeking out its quarry by swimming underwater. It spears a fish with its beak, surfaces, tosses the fish into the air, catches it, and gulps it down head first. During this activity, the anhinga has gotten soaked to the skin, for, unlike ducks and many other water birds, it is not well supplied with oil to keep its plumage dry. So, following a plunge, the anhinga struggles to the branch of a shrub or tree, and, spreading its wings, hangs its feathers out to dry.

The snail kite, one of America's rarest birds, flies low over the fresh-water marshes, its head pointed downward, searching for its sole food—the Pomacea snail. A sharply hooked beak enables it to remove the snail from its shell. More striking in appearance is its cousin, the swallow-tailed kite, aerial acrobat of the hawk family—a migrant that nests in the park in spring and spends the winter in South America. On long, pointed wings this

65

LITTLE BLUE HERON

immature   adult

GREAT BLUE HERON

WHITE PHASE

REDDISH EGRET

WOOD STORK

WHITE IBIS

GLOSSY IBIS

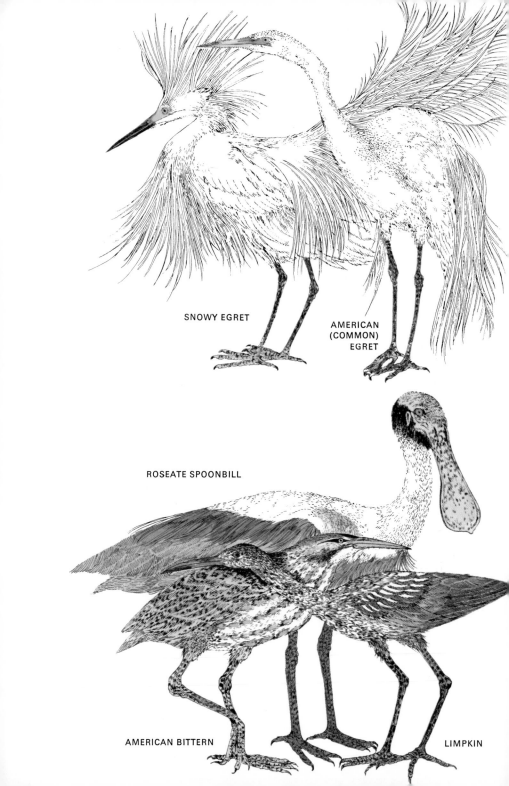

SNOWY EGRET

AMERICAN
(COMMON)
EGRET

ROSEATE SPOONBILL

AMERICAN BITTERN

LIMPKIN

handsome bird eats in the air while holding itself in one place on the wind. In the mangroves, it hunts in an unusual way : skimming over the trees, it snatches lizards and other small animals from the topmost branches. Red-shouldered hawks, often seen perching on the treetops beside the park road, feed upon snakes and other small animals. The fish-eating osprey is another conspicuous resident of the park, and its bulky nests will be seen when you take a boat trip into Florida Bay or the mangrove wilderness. The bald eagle, which, sadly, is no longer common in North America and may soon be exterminated because of pesticide pollution of its fishing waters, is still holding out in the Ever-glades region, where 50 or so breeding pairs seem to be reproducing successfully.

The long-legged wading birds of the heron family are so numerous and so much alike in appear-ance that you will need your bird guide for sure identification. The waders are interesting to watch, because of the variety of feeding methods. Particularly amusing are the antics of the reddish egret as it hunts small animals in the shallows of Florida Bay at low tide. It is much unlike other herons in its manner of hunting : it lurches through the shallows, dashing to left and right as if drunk, in pursuit of its prey. This clownish survivor of the old plume-hunting days exists in Florida in very limited numbers.

Since about 300 species of birds have been record-ed in the park, this sampling barely suggests the pleasures awaiting you if you plan to spend some time playing the Everglades bird-watching game.

Reptiles and Amphibians

Everglades' most famous citizen—the alligator—
is looked for by all visitors to the park, who may,
however, be unaware that many other kinds of
reptiles and a dozen species of amphibians dwell here.

The American crocodile, less common than the
alligator and restricted to the Florida Bay region,
is a shy and secretive animal seen by few visitors.
Similar in size and appearance to the alligator, it
is distinguished by a narrower snout and a lighter
color. Its habitat overlaps that of the alligator,
which prefers fresh or brackish water.

The turtles of the park include terrestrial, fresh-water,
and marine species. Box turtles are often seen
along the roads. The softshell and snapping turtles
live in the fresh-water areas and are often eaten by
alligators. Loggerhead turtles nest on Cape Sable
beaches ; otherwise they rarely come ashore. Their
eggs are often discovered and devoured by the
abundant raccoons. But man has been largely re-
sponsible for the loggerhead's increasing rarity.

Although the park has about two dozen species of
snakes, you may not encounter any of them. Most
are harmless—several species of snakes frequent
the waterways, and it is a mistake to assume that
any water snake you see is a moccasin. Two worth
watching for are the everglades rat snake and the
indigo snake, both handsome and entirely harmless
to man. The former is a constrictor, feeding mostly
on rodents. The indigo is one of our longest snakes—
sometimes reaching more than 100 inches—and now
in danger of extinction.

Ordinary caution and alertness when walking on
trails is advisable ; but keep in mind that the snakes
are not aggressive, and that as part of the web of
life in the park they are given protection just as
are birds and mammals.

70   Of those close relatives of snakes, the lizards, the

Florida anole is most commonly seen. This is the little reptile sold at circuses as a "chameleon"; it is quite unlike the true chameleon of the Old World. The so-called "glass snake"—which got its name from its defensive maneuver of dropping off its tail (which is longer than the rest of its body) and from its snakelike appearance—is actually a legless lizard. The lizards, like the smaller snakes, are primarily insectivorous.

The park's amphibians, too, are quite inconspicuous. The voices of frogs and toads during the breeding season, however, are part of the Everglades atmosphere. You will enjoy the nocturnal serenade at egg-laying time—and it is quite possible to learn to identify species by their songs, which are as distinctive as those of birds.

The green treefrog, with its bell-like, repeated "queenk-queenk-queenk" call, is abundant, and can be seen and heard easily during the breeding season, particularly at Royal Palm Hammock and on the Anhinga Trail.

The cold-blooded vertebrates, including fish, amphibians, and reptiles, play a significant role in the balance of life in the park, feeding upon each other and upon lesser animals and in turn being food for larger predators such as herons, hawks, raccoons, and otters.

Fishes

"Fishing Reserved for the Birds," says the sign at the beginning of the Anhinga Trail. Actually, the catching of fish in the fresh waters of the park is an important activity not only for herons, anhingas, grebes, and ospreys, but also for raccoons, mink, turtles, alligators . . . and bigger fish. Not surprisingly in the drowned habitats of Everglades, even the smallest fish are important in the web of life.

One tiny species, the gambusia, is of special interest to us. This 2-inch fish is credited with helping keep down the numbers of mosquitoes by feeding upon their aquatic larvae. This accounts for its other name—mosquito fish—and for its popularity with humans. But its services to us are not the measure of the gambusia's importance, for it is a link in many food chains in the park's brackish and fresh-water habitats. Beginning with algae, we can trace one such chain through mosquito larvae, sunfish, and bass, to end with the alligator. We can only guess at the extent of the ecological effects of the loss of a single species such as the little gambusia.

The larger fish of Everglades are the most sought after. Sport fishermen want to know where to find and how to recognize the many varieties of game fish, especially largemouth bass and such famed salt-water and brackish zone species as tarpon, snook, mangrove snapper, and barracuda. Because of its cycles of flood and drought, and the shifting brackish zones, however, the distribution and the numbers of fish fluctuate greatly in the glades and mangrove regions. At times of drought, the fish concentrations are particularly evident. In mid- or late winter, sloughs that are no longer deep enough to flow, pools, and other standing bodies of water will have a myriad of gambusia, killifish, and minnows. Larger fish seek the sanctuary of the headwaters of the Harney, Shark, and Broad Rivers. At such times concentrations of bass may be so great that the angler may catch his daily limit in a few hours. (There are no legal limits for the herons and 'gators!)

As water levels continue to fall, salt water intrudes farther inland; such species as snook and tarpon move up the now brackish rivers, and may be seen in the same waters as bluegills and largemouth bass.

In some years water levels drop so severely that concentrations of fish are too great for the habitat to support. As the surface water shrinks, the fish use up the available free oxygen and begin to die. The largest expire first; the smaller fish seem less vulnerable to depleted oxygen supply. Even though many tons of fish may perish in such a die-off, a few small specimens of each variety survive to restock the glades when the rains return.

With no cold season when fish must remain dormant, and with a year-round food supply, bass and sun-fish grow rapidly and reach breeding size before the next drought.

These fish kills are associated with drought con-ditions that occur in the ordinary course of events, and thus are natural phenomena not to be considered ecological disasters. But man's violent upsetting of the drainage patterns of south Florida, through airport, canal, and highway construction and other developments, can bring about such drastic shortages (or even surpluses) of water that irrep-arable damage could be done to the ecology of Everglades aquatic communities.

While fish watching may not be the exciting sport that bird watching is, you are the loser if you ignore this part of the life of Everglades. Fish are so abundant in the park that no one has to haul them in on a line to discover them. You can hardly miss spotting the larger fresh-water forms if you take the trouble to look down into the sloughs, ponds, and alligator holes.

Identifying the species of fish, however, is more
73   difficult. The voracious-looking Florida spotted gar

is an exception. This important predator on smaller fishes, which is in turn a major item in the diet of the alligator, is quite easily recognized. Experienced anglers will spot the largemouthed bass and the bluegill sunfish. You'll see these and others as you walk on the Anhinga Trail boardwalk.

As you watch alligators and other native Everglades predators, you may get an inkling of how important in the web of life are the prolific fish populations of the sloughs, marshes, swamps, and offshore waters of the park.

Animals without Backbones

Insects are the most noticeable of the park's invertebrates. (At times you may find your can of repellent as important as your shoes!) In all the fresh-water and brackish environments, insects and their larvae are important links in the food chains— at the beginning as primary consumers of algae and other plant material, and farther along as predators, mostly on other insects. Some insects are parasites on the park's warmblooded animals (including you).

The invertebrates most sought by visitors are molluscs—or rather, their shells. You may find a few on the beach at Cape Sable, but don't expect to find the park a productive shelling area. Stick to marine shells—*dead* ones. You cannot collect the fresh-water molluscs. Also protected are the tree snails of jungle hammocks. Famed for their beauty, these snails of the genus *Liguus*, which grow to as much as 2½ inches in diameter, feed upon the lichens growing on certain hammock trees. Look for them—but leave them undisturbed, for they are a part of the community, protected just as are the park's royal palms and its alligators.

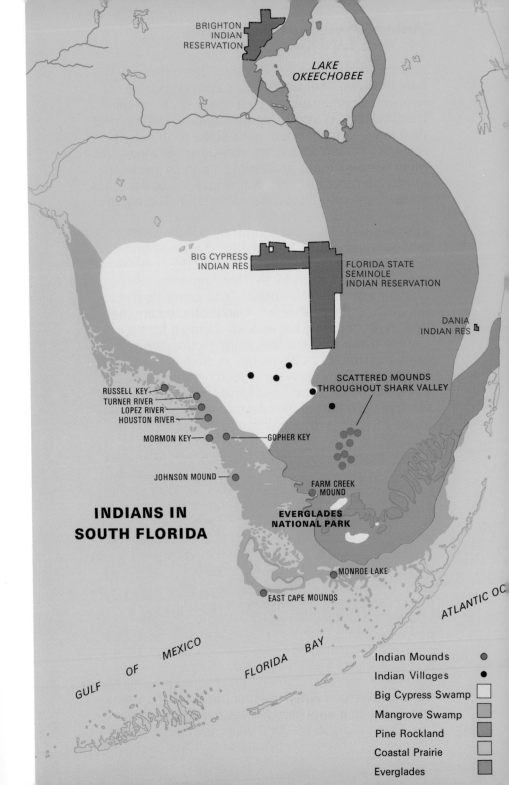

BRIGHTON
INDIAN
RESERVATION

*LAKE
OKEECHOBEE*

BIG CYPRESS
INDIAN RES

FLORIDA STATE
SEMINOLE
INDIAN RESERVATION

DANIA
INDIAN RES

SCATTERED MOUNDS
THROUGHOUT SHARK VALLEY

RUSSELL KEY
TURNER RIVER
LOPEZ RIVER
HOUSTON RIVER

MORMON KEY — GOPHER KEY

JOHNSON MOUND

**INDIANS IN
SOUTH FLORIDA**

**EVERGLADES
NATIONAL PARK**

FARM CREEK
MOUND

MONROE LAKE

EAST CAPE MOUNDS

ATLANTIC OC

GULF   OF   MEXICO   FLORIDA   BAY

Indian Mounds

Indian Villages

Big Cypress Swamp

Mangrove Swamp

Pine Rockland

Coastal Prairie

Everglades

INDIANS
OF THE EVERGLADES

Your first awareness of the south Florida Indians will probably come during a trip along the Tamiami Trail (U.S. 41, the cross-State highway just north of the park). You will notice clusters of Indian homes close to the road. Some are built on stilts, are thatched with palm fronds, and are open-sided so that no walls hamper the flow of cooling breezes. Many of the glades Indians prefer to live as their ancestors did some 150 years ago when they were newcomers to the everglades. Others have adopted the white man's dwellings (as well as his occupations).

The Indians of south Florida—Miccosukees, sometimes called "Trail Indians"; and Muskogees, the "Cow Creek Seminoles"—are separate tribes, not sharing a common language. Today no Indians live inside the park boundaries.

The Indians arrived in Spanish Florida after the American Revolution. Many Creeks of Georgia and Alabama, crowded by the aggressive white man, fled south to the peninsula. They first settled in north Florida; when Florida became a State in 1845 they had to retreat farther south. Driven into the interior during the Seminole War of 1835, they eventually settled in the everglades, where deer, fish, and fruit were available. Though their territory is now much more limited, they still retain much of their independent spirit, and have never signed a peace treaty with the U.S. Government.

Many earn their living operating air boats, as proprietors and employees of roadside businesses, and in a variety of jobs on farms and in cities. The women create distinctive handicraft items, which find a ready market with tourists.

No one is certain when the first Indians—the Calusas and Tequestas—appeared in south Florida; it may have been more than 2,000 years ago. Even more

than today's glades Indians, these coastal Indians lived with the rhythm of river and tides, rain and drought. Hunting, fishing, and gathering of shellfish were their means of existence. We have learned this much of their life from artifacts unearthed from the many Indian mounds or washed up along the beaches. They lived on huge shell mounds, made pottery, used sharks' teeth to make saws, and fashioned other tools from conch shells. They even built impoundments for fish—a few remains of these can be seen today. They were ingenious hunters. (Ponce de León and his Spanish explorer-marauders were said to have been turned back from the everglades by the deadly arrows these Indians fashioned from rushes.)

Following the arrival of the Spanish, these early Indians disappeared from the scene. They were apparently wiped out, destroyed by the white man's diseases as much as by his aggression; but some may have escaped to Cuba. Perhaps a handful of them were still in the everglades when the Creeks came down from the north in 1835, and were absorbed into the new tribe. Their known history ends here.

Proud, independent, and ingenious in wresting a living from the land and the water, the Indians knew how to live with nature.   Unlike the white man, they fitted into the plant-and-animal communities. Today these communities have been severely disrupted. In the few decades that the white man has been "developing" the region, he has broken every chain of life described in this book.

Alligator populations have been much reduced in south Florida ; their chief prey, the garfish, has in some places become so numerous as to constitute a nuisance (most of all to the fresh-water anglers, some of whom had a hand in the killing of alligators). The pattern of waterflow over the glades, through the cypress swamps, and into the mangrove wilderness has been altered by highways and canals. Much of the habitat has been wiped out by construction of homes and factories and by farming operations.   An increasingly alarming development is the pollution of glades waters by agricultural chemicals.

Only through complete understanding of this fragile, unique subtropical world can man reverse the destructive trend.   Only through carefully applied protective and management practices can we make progress toward restoring to the Everglades some of its lost splendor.

Glossary

ALGAE: (pronounced "AL-jee") A group of plants (singular: ALGA, pronounced "AL-ga"), one-celled or many-celled, having chlorophyll, without roots, and living in damp places or in water.

BRACKISH WATER: Mixed fresh and salt water. Many species of plants and animals of marine and fresh-water habitats are adapted to life in estuaries and coastal swamps and marshes, where the water varies greatly in degree of salinity. Some animal species can be found in all three habitats.

BROMELIAD: A plant of the pineapple family. Many bromeliads are air plants, growing (not parasitically) on the trunks and branches of other plants, or even, as in the case of "Spanish moss," on telephone wires.

COMMUNITY: The living part of the ecosystem; an assemblage of plants and animals living in a particular area or physical habitat. It can be as small as a decaying log, with its variety of mosses, insect larvae, burrowing beetles, ants, etc.; or as large as a forest of hundreds of square miles.

DECIDUOUS TREES: Trees that shed their leaves annually. Most hardwood trees are deciduous; some conifers, such as larches and baldcypresses, are deciduous.

ECOLOGY: The study of the relationship of living things to one another and to their physical environment.

ENDANGERED: A species of plant or animal that, throughout all or a significant portion of its range, is in danger of extinction.

ENVIRONMENT: All the external conditions, such as soil, water, air, and organisms, surrounding a living thing.

ESTIVATION: A prolonged dormant or sleeplike state that enables an animal to survive the summer in a hot climate. As in hibernation, breathing and heartbeat slow down, and the animal neither eats nor drinks.

ESTUARY: The portion of a river or coastal wetland affected by the rise and fall of the tide, containing a graded mixture of fresh and salt water.

EVERGLADE: A tract of marshy land covered in places with tall grasses. (In this book, "the everglades" refers to the river of grass; "Everglades" refers to the park, which contains other habitats besides everglades.)

EXOTIC: A foreign plant or animal that has been introduced, intentionally or unintentionally, into a new area.

FOOD CHAIN: A series of plants and animals linked by their food relationships, beginning with a green plant and ending with a predator.

HABITAT: The place where an organism lives; the immediate surroundings, living and unliving, of an organism. The habitat of the pine warbler is the pinelands; the habitat of an internal parasite of this bird is the body of the warbler.

HAMMOCK: A dense growth of broad-leaved trees on a slightly elevated area, not wet enough to be a swamp. In the park, hammocks are surrounded either by pineland or by marshland (glades).

HARDWOOD TREES: Trees with broad leaves (as opposed to conebearing trees, which have needles or scales). Most hardwood trees are deciduous, though many in south Florida retain their leaves throughout the year.

KEY: A reef or low-lying island. In south Florida, the term "key" is often also applied to hammocks or pinelands, which occupy areas where the limestone is raised above the surrounding wetlands.

LIMESTONE: A sedimentary rock derived from the shells and skeletons of animals deposited in seas, and consisting mostly of calcium carbonate. Soluble in water having a slight degree of acidity, it is often characterized by caverns and, in the everglades, by a very pitted surface. The rock underlying most of the park is the Miami Oölite (pronounced OH-uh-lite), formed during a recent glacial period. Oölitic limestone is composed of tiny round concretions, only indirectly derived from marine shells.

MANGROVE: Any of a group of tropical or subtropical trees, growing in estuaries and other low-lying coastal areas, usually producing aerial roots or prop roots and often forming dense growths over a large area. In south Florida there are four species, belonging to three different families.

MARSH: A wetland, salt or fresh, where few if any trees and shrubs grow, characterized by grasses and sedges; in fresh-water marshes, cattails are common.

MARL: In this book, used in the sense of a deposit of mixed limestone and smaller amounts of clay; south Florida marls are sometimes called lime muds.

PEAT: Partly decayed, moisture-absorbing plant matter accumulated in bogs, swamps, etc.

PREDATOR: An animal that lives by capturing other animals for food.

SLOUGH: A channel of slow-moving water in coastal marshland. The Shark River Slough and Taylor Slough are the main channels where the glades water flows in the park. Generally remaining as reservoirs of water when the glades dry in the rainless season, they are important to survival of aquatic animals.

SWAMP: Wetland characterized by shrubs or trees such as maples, gums, baldcypresses, and, in south Florida coast areas, mangroves. Fresh-water swamps are usually not covered by water the year around.

THREATENED: A species still present in its range but that, without significant changes in conditions, is capable of becoming endangered.

TREE ISLAND: An island of trees, shrubs, and herbaceous plants growing on an elevation, in a depression, or at the same level as the surrounding glades. Includes hammocks, willow heads, cypress heads, and bayheads.

For Reading and Reference

Carmichael, Pete, and Winston Williams. *Florida's Fabulous Reptiles and Amphibians*. Tampa: World Publications, 1991.

Cox, W. Eugene. *In Pictures—Everglades: The Continuing Story*. Las Vegas: KC Publications, 1989.

Craighead, Frank C. *The Role of the Alligator in Shaping Plant Communities and Maintaining Wildlife in the Southern Everglades*. Maitland: Florida Audubon Society.*

de Golia, Jack. *Everglades: The Story Behind the Scenery*. Las Vegas: KC Publications, 1981.

Douglas, Marjory Stoneman. *Everglades: River of Grass*. Marietta, Georgia: Mockingbird Books, 1974. Revised Edition also available: Sarasota: Pineapple Press, 1988.

Downs, Dorothy. *Art of the Florida Seminole and Miccosukee Indians*. Gainesville: University Press of Florida, 1995.

Gingerich, Jerry Lee. *Florida's Fabulous Mammals*. Tampa: World Publications, 1994.

Hoffmeister, John Edward. *Land From Sea: The Geologic Story of South Florida*. Coral Gables: University of Miami Press, 1968.

Kale, Herbert W., and David Maehr. *Florida's Birds*. Sarasota: Pineapple Press, 1990.

Kern, Rich. *Video: The Everglades*. Miami: Rich Kern Nature Series, 1992.

Lodge, Thomas E. *The Everglades Handbook: Understanding the Ecosystem*. Delray Beach: St. Lucie Press. 1994.

Loughlin, Maureen H., compiler. *Everglades National Park Bird Checklist/Habitat Guide*. Homestead: Florida National Parks and Monuments Association, Inc., 1991.

Peterson, Roger Tory. *A Field Guide to the Birds of Eastern and Central North America*. Boston: Houghton Mifflin Company, 1980.

Ripple, Jeff. *Big Cypress Swamp and the Ten Thousand Islands*. Columbia: University of South Carolina Press, 1992.

Robertson, William B. *Everglades: The Park Story.* Homestead: Florida National Parks and Monuments Association, Inc., 1989.

Romashko, Sandra. *The Shell Book.* Miami: Windward Publishing, Inc., 1984.

Seavey, Jean. *Native Trees of South Florida. Plants (Wildflowers) of South Florida.* (Plastic ID Cards) Homestead: Field Guides, 1995.

Stevenson, George B. *Trees of the Everglades National Park and the Florida Keys.* Homestead: Florida National Parks and Monuments Association, Inc., 1992.

Tebeau, Charlton W. *Man in the Everglades.* Coral Gables: University of Miami Press, 1968.

Toops, Connie *The Alligator: Monarch of the Marsh.* Homestead: Florida National Parks and Monuments Association, Inc., 1988.

Toops, Connie. *Everglades.* Stillwater, Minnesota: Voyageur Press, 1989.

Truesdell, William G. *A Guide to the Wilderness Waterway of the Everglades National Park.* Coral Gables: University of Miami Press, 1985.

U.S. Fish and Wildlife Service. *Rare and Endangered Fish and Wildlife of the United States.* Washington: U.S. Government Printing Office.*

Williams, Winston. *Florida's Fabulous Waterbirds.* Tampa: World Publications, 1984.

Zim, Herbert S. *Everglades National Park and the Nearby Florida Keys.* New York: Golden Press, 1992 edition. Distributed by Florida National Parks and Monuments Association, Inc.

All references, except those asterisked, are available from Florida National Parks and Monuments Association, 10 Parachute Key #51, Homestead, FL 33034. Phone 305-247-1216.

Rare and Endangered Animals

Here is a partial list of the rare and endangered species and subspecies found in Everglades National Park and Fort Jefferson National Monument.

Mammals
Florida Panther (Cougar)
West Indian Manatee (Sea Cow)

Birds
Snail Kite
Southern Bald Eagle
Arctic Peregrine Falcon
Cape Sable Sparrow
Wood Stork
Red-cockaded Woodpecker

Reptiles and Amphibians
Green Turtle
Eastern Indigo Snake
Hawksbill Turtle
Loggerhead Turtle
American Crocodile

Checklist of Mammals

More than 40 species of mammals are found in Everglades National Park. Many of them are species commonly associated with drier habitats that have adapted to the semi-aquatic environment that comprises most of the park. It is not uncommon to see whitetail deer wading through the sawgrass prairie or a bobcat foraging for food in a mangrove swamp. This list is made up of species found within the boundary of the park or in the immediate area. Species considered exotic to Everglades National Park are marked with an asterisk (*).

Oposum   *Didelphis marsupialis*
Short-tailed shrew   *Blarina brevicauda*
Least shrew   *Cryptotis parva*
Evening bat   *Nycticeius hymeralis*
Brazilian free-tailed bat   *Tadarida brasiliensis*
Nine-banded armadillo   *Dasypus novemcinctus**
Marsh rabbit   *Sylvilagus palustris*
Eastern cottontail   *Sylvilagus floridanus*
Gray squirrel   *Sciurus carolinensis*
Fox squirrel   *Sciurus niger*
Southern flying squirrel   *Glaucomys volans*
Rice rat   *Oryzomys palustris*
Cotton mouse   *Peromyscus gossypinus*
Cotton rat   *Sigmodon hispisus*
Roundtail muskrat   *Neofiber alleni*
Roof rat   *Rattus rattus**
Norway rat   *Rattus norvegicus*
House mouse   *Mus musculus**
Atlantic bottlenosed dolphin   *Tursiops truncatus*
Short-finned, or Pilot, whale   *Globicephala marcorhyncha*
Gray fox   *Urocyon cineroargenteus*
Red fox   *Vulpes vulpes**
Domestic dog   *Canis familiaris**
Black bear   *Ursus americanus*
Raccoon   *Procyon lotor*
Coati   *Nasua narica**
Everglades mink   *Mustela vison*
Long-tailed weasel   *Mustela frenata*
Eastern spotted skunk   *Spirogale putorius*
Striped skunk   *Mephitis mephitis*
River otter   *Lutra canadensis*
Florida panther   *Felis concolor coryi*
Bobcat   *Lynx rufus*
Domestic cat   *Felis domesticus**
West Indian Manatee   *Trichechus manatus*
Domestic pig   *Sus scrofa**
Whitetail deer   *Odocoileus virginia*

Checklist of Birds

This is a complete list of the birds known in the park—347 species as of June 1, 1985—along with a key indicating the abundance and seasonal occurrence of each species. As noted in this list many birds are known in the park from only a few sightings. A few are exotic birds that have escaped captivity. Species considered exotic to Everglades Park are marked with an asterisk (*). Users can contribute to updating future lists by carefully recording details of their observations of less common species and reporting that information to park personnel. For purposes of this listing the seasons are as follows:

Spring: March 1 to May 31
Summer: June 1 to July 31
Fall: August 1 to November 15
Winter: November 16 to February 28

Key to Checklist
C Common
U Uncommon
R Rare
F Fewer than 10 sightings
B Breeds in park
? Uncertain if species breeds in park

Name of Bird	Breeds in park	Spring	Summer	Fall	Winter
Red-throated Loon					F
Common Loon		R		R	R
Pied-billed Grebe	B	C	U	C	C
Horned Grebe		C		C	C
Red-necked Grebe					F
Sooty Shearwater			F		
Wilson's Storm Petrel			F		
Brown Booby			F		
Northern Gannet		F		F	F
American White Pelican		C	R	C	C
Brown Pelican	B	C	C	C	C
Great Cormorant					F
Double-crested Cormorant	B	C	C	C	C
Anhinga	B	C	C	C	C
Magnificent Frigatebird		U	U	U	U
American Bittern	?	U	R	U	C
Least Bittern	B	U	U	U	U
Great Blue Heron	B	C	C	C	C
Great Blue Heron (White phase)	B	C	C	C	C
Great Egret	B	C	C	C	C
Snowy Egret	B	C	C	C	C

88

Name of Bird	Breeds in park	Spring	Summer	Fall	Winter
Little Blue Heron	B	C	C	C	C
Tricolored Heron	B	C	C	C	C
Reddish Egret	B	U	U	U	U
Cattle Egret	B	C	C	C	C
Green-backed Heron	B	C	C	C	C
Black-crowned Night Heron	B	C	C	C	C
Yellow-crowned Night Heron	B	U	U	U	U
White Ibis	B	C	C	C	C
Scarlet Ibis (probably escapes)		R	R	R	R
Glossy Ibis	B	U	U	U	U
White-faced Ibis				F	
Roseate Spoonbill	B	C	U	C	C
Wood Stork	B	U	R	U	U
Great Flamingo (probably escapes)		R	R	R	R
Fulvous Whistling Duck		U	U	U	U
Snow Goose					F
Snow Goose (Blue Phase)					F
Brant					F
Canada Goose					F
Wood Duck					R
Green-winged Teal		U		R	U
American Black Duck					F
Mottled Duck	B	C	C	C	C
Mallard					R
White-checked Pintail		F			F
Northern Pintail		C		R	C
Blue-winged Teal		C	R	C	C
Cinnamon Teal		F			
Northern Shoveler		C	R	C	C
Gadwall		R			R
Eurasian Wigeon					F
American Wigeon		C		C	C
Canvasback		R			R
Redhead		R			R
Ring-necked Duck		C		C	C
Greater Scaup					F
Lesser Scaup		C		C	C
Oldsquaw					F
Black Scoter					F
Surf Scoter					F
Common Goldeneye					F
Bufflehead					R
Hooded Merganser		U		R	U
Red-breasted Merganser		C	R	C	C
Ruddy Duck		U		U	C
Masked Duck					F
Black Vulture	B	C	C	C	C

Name of Bird	Breeds in park	Spring	Summer	Fall	Winter
Turkey Vulture	B	C	C	C	C
Osprey	B	C	C	C	C
American Swallow-tailed Kite	B	C	C	R	
Black-shouldered Kite		R	R		
Snail Kite	B	R	R	R	R
Mississippi Kite		F		F	
Bald Eagle	B	C	C	C	C
Northern Harrier		U		U	C
Sharp-shinned Hawk		U		U	U
Cooper's Hawk		R		R	R
Red-shouldered Hawk	B	C	C	C	C
Broad-winged Hawk		U		U	U
Short-tailed Hawk	B	U	R	U	U
Swainson's Hawk		R		R	U
Red-tailed Hawk	B	U	U	U	U
Rough-legged Hawk					F
Golden Eagle					F
Crested Caracara					F
American Kestrel		C		C	C
Merlin		U		U	U
Peregrine Falcon		U		U	U
Wild Turkey	B	R	R	R	R
Northern Bobwhite	B	C	C	C	C
Yellow Rail					F
Black Rail					R
Clapper Rail	B	C	C	C	C
King Rail	B	C	C	C	C
Virginia Rail		R		R	R
Sora Rail		C		C	C
Purple Gallinule	B	C	C	C	C
Common Moorhen	B	C	C	C	C
American Coot	B	C	R	C	C
Caribbean Coot		F		F	F
Limpkin	B	C	C	C	C
Sandhill Crane	B	R	R	R	R
Black-bellied Plover		C	R	C	C
Lesser Golden Plover		R		R	R
Snowy Plover			F		F
Wilson's Plover	B	C	C	C	U
Semipalmated Plover		C	U	C	C
Piping Plover		U		U	U
Killdeer	B	C	U	C	C
American Oystercatcher					R
Black-necked Stilt	B	U	R	U	R
American Avocet		C	U	C	C
Greater Yellowlegs		C	U	C	C
Lesser Yellowlegs		C	U	C	C
Solitary Sandpiper		U		U	R
Willet	?	C	U	C	C
Spotted Sandpiper		C		C	C
Upland Sandpiper		F		F	

Name of Bird	Breeds in park	Spring	Summer	Fall	Winter
Whimbrel		U	R	U	U
Long-billed Curlew		R		R	R
Hudsonian Godwit		F			F
Marbled Godwit		C	R	C	C
Ruddy Turnstone		C	U	C	C
Red Knot		U	R	U	U
Sanderling		U		U	U
Semipalmated Sandpiper		U		U	R
Western Sandpiper		C	R	C	C
Least Sandpiper		C	U	C	C
White-rumped Sandpiper		R	R		
Baird's Sandpiper				R	
Pectoral Sandpiper		C		C	R
Sharp-tailed Sandpiper				F	
Dunlin		C		C	C
Curlew Sandpiper					F
Stilt Sandpiper			U	U	R
Buff-breasted Sandpiper				F	
Ruff				F	
Short-billed Dowitcher		C	U	C	C
Long-billed Dowitcher		U	U	U	R
Common Snipe		U		U	U
American Woodcock		R			R
Wilson's Phalarope				F	
Red-necked Phalarope				F	
Parasitic Jaeger					F
Laughing Gull	B	C	C	C	C
Franklin's Gull					F
Bonaparte's Gull		U			U
Ring-billed Gull		C	U	C	C
Herring Gull		C	U	C	C
Lesser Black-backed Gull					F
Great Black-backed Gull					F
Gull-billed Tern		U	U	U	U
Caspian Tern		C	R	C	C
Royal Tern		C	U	C	C
Sandwich Tern		U	U	U	U
Roseate Tern					R
Common Tern		U		U	U
Forster's Tern		C	U	C	C
Least Tern	B	C	C	U	
Bridled Tern			F		
Sooty Tern			F	F	
Black Tern		U	U	U	R
Brown Noddy			F	F	
Black Skimmer		C	C	C	C
Rock Dove*		F	F	F	F
White-crowned Pigeon	B	C	C	C	U
White-winged Dove		F	F	F	F
Zenaida Dove			F		
Mourning Dove	B	C	C	C	C

91

Name of Bird	Breeds in park	Spring	Summer	Fall	Winter
Common Ground Dove	B	U	U	U	U
Key West Quail Dove		F			F
Budgerigar (escapes)		F			F
Rose-ringed Parakeet (escapes)			F		
Monk Parakeet (escapes)		F			
Canary-winged Parakeet (escapes)		F			
Yellow-billed Cuckoo	B	C	C	C	R
Mangrove Cuckoo	B	U	U	U	U
Smooth-billed Ani	B	U	U	U	U
Groove-billed Ani		F	F		F
Common Barn Owl	B	U	U	U	U
Eastern Screech Owl	B	C	C	C	C
Great Horned Owl	B	R	R	R	R
Burrowing Owl					R
Barred Owl	B	C	C	C	C
Long-eared Owl					F
Short-eared Owl		R		R	R
Lesser Nighthawk		F			F
Common Nighthawk	B	C	C	C	R
Chuck-will's-widow	B	C	C	C	R
Whip-poor-will		U		U	C
Chimney Swift				R	
Ruby-throated Hummingbird		C	R	C	C
Belted Kingfisher		C	R	C	C
Red-headed Woodpecker					F
Red-bellied Woodpecker	B	C	C	C	C
Yellow-bellied Sapsucker		U		U	C
Downy Woodpecker	B	U	U	U	U
Hairy Woodpecker	B	R	R	R	R
Red-cockaded Woodpecker		Extirpated			
Northern Flicker	B	C	C	C	C
Pileated Woodpecker	B	C	C	C	C
Ivory-billed Woodpecker		Extirpated			
Olive-sided Flycatcher				F	
Eastern Wood Pewee		U		U	R
Acadian Flycatcher				R	
Willow Flycatcher				R	
Least Flycatcher		U	U	U	R
Eastern Phoebe		C		C	C
Say's Phoebe					F
Vermilion Flycatcher		F			F
Great Crested Flycatcher	B	C	C	C	C
Brown-crested Flycatcher		R			R
Tropical Kingbird		F			F
Western Kingbird		U		U	U
Eastern Kingbird	B	C	C	C	R

Name of Bird	Breeds in park	Spring	Summer	Fall	Winter
Gray Kingbird	B	C	C	C	
Scissor-tailed Flycatcher		R		R	R
Purple Martin		C	C	C	
Tree Swallow		C		C	C
Northern Rough-winged Swallow		U		U	R
Bank Swallow		U		U	
Cliff Swallow		R		U	
Barn Swallow	B	U	R	C	R
Blue Jay	B	C	C	C	C
American Crow	B	C	C	C	C
Fish Crow					F
Tufted Titmouse		R			R
White-breasted Nuthatch					F
Brown-headed Nuthatch		Extirpated			
Brown Creeper					F
Carolina Wren	B	C	C	C	C
House Wren		C		C	C
Winter Wren					F
Sedge Wren		U		U	U
Marsh Wren		U		U	U
Ruby-crowned Kinglet		U		U	U
Blue-gray Gnatcatcher		C		C	C
Eastern Bluebird		Extirpated			
Veery		U		U	
Gray-cheeked Thrush		U		U	
Swainson's Thrush		U		U	F
Hermit Thrush		U		U	R
Wood Thrush		R		R	F
American Robin					R-C
Gray Catbird		C		C	C
Northern Mockingbird	B	C	C	C	C
Brown Thrasher		U		U	U
Water Pipit				R	R
Cedar Waxwing		R-C		R-C	R-C
Loggerhead Shrike	B	U	U	U	U
European Starling*	B	U	U	U	U
Hill Myna (probably escapes)		F			
Thick-billed Vireo					F
White-eyed Vireo	B	C	C	C	C
Bell's Vireo				F	F
Solitary Vireo		U		U	U
Yellow-throated Vireo		U		U	U
Warbling Vireo		F		F	
Philadelphia Vireo		R		R	
Red-eyed Vireo		C		C	F
Black-whispered Vireo	B	C	C	C	
Blue-winged Warbler		R		R	F
Golden-winged Warbler		R		R	
Tennessee Warbler		U		U	R

Name of Bird	Breeds in park	Spring	Summer	Fall	Winter
Orange-crowned Warbler		U		U	U
Nashville Warbler		F		R	F
Northern Parula		C	R	C	C
Yellow Warbler	B	C	C	C	U
Chestnut-sided Warbler		R		R	
Magnolia Warbler		U		U	R
Cape May Warbler		U-C		U-C	R
Black-throated Blue Warbler		C		C	U-R
Yellow-rumped Warbler		R-C		R-C	C
Black-throated Gray Warbler					F
Black-throated Green Warbler		U		U	U
Blackburnian Warbler		U		U	F
Yellow-throated Warbler		C	U	C	C
Pine Warbler	B	C	C	C	C
Kirtland's Warbler					F
Prairie Warbler	B	C	C	C	C
Palm Warbler		C		C	C
Bay-breasted Warbler				F	F
Blackpoll Warbler		C		R	
Cerulean Warbler				R	
Black-and-white Warbler		C		C	C
American Redstart		C	U	C	U
Prothonotary Warbler		U		U	F
Worm-eating Warbler		U		U	R
Swainson's Warbler		R		R	
Ovenbird		C		C	C
Northern Waterthrush		C		C	C
Louisiana Waterthrush		C	U	C	R
Kentucky Warbler		R		R	F
Connecticut Warbler		R			
Mourning Warbler		F			
Common Yellowthroat	B	C	C	C	C
Hooded Warbler		U		U	F
Wilson's Warbler		R		R	F
Yellow-breasted Chat		U		U	U
Bananaquit				F	
Stripe-headed Tanager					F
Summer Tanager		R		R	F
Scarlet Tanager		F		F	F
Western Tanager		F		F	F
Northern Cardinal	B	C	C	C	C
Rose-breasted Grosbeak		U		U	R
Blue Grosbeak		U		U	F
Indigo Bunting		C		C	R
Painted Bunting		C		C	U-R
Dickcissel		F		F	F
Rufous-sided Towhee	B	C	C	C	C
Black-faced Grassquit			F	F	

Name of Bird	Breeds in park	Spring	Summer	Fall	Winter
Bachman's Sparrow		F		F	F
Chipping Sparrow		R		R	R
Clay-colored Sparrow		R		R	R
Field Sparrow		U		U	U
Vesper Sparrow		F		F	F
Lark Sparrow				F	F
Lark Bunting			F		F
Savannah Sparrow		C		C	C
Grasshopper Sparrow		U		U	U
Le Conte's Sparrow					F
Sharp-tailed Sparrow		R		R	U
Seaside Sparrow					R
Cape Sable Seaside Sparrow	B	C	C	C	C
Song Sparrow					F
Lincoln's Sparrow					R-U
Swamp Sparrow		C		C	C
White-throated Sparrow				F	F
White-crowned Sparrow				R	F
Dark-eyed Junco				F	F
Bobolink		C		C	F
Red-winged Blackbird	B	C	C	C	C
Eastern Meadowlark	B	C	C	C	C
Yellow-headed Blackbird		R		R	R
Rusty Blackbird					F
Brewer's Blackbird					R
Boat-tailed Grackle	B	C	C	C	C
Common Grackle	B	C	C	C	C
Bronzed Cowbird					F
Brown-headed Cowbird		U		U	R
Orchard Oriole		U		U	
Spot-breasted Oriole		F			
Northern Oriole (Baltimore race)		C		C	R
Northern Oriole (Bullock's race)		R		R	R
Pine Siskin					F
American Goldfinch		C		C	C
House Sparrow*	B	U	U	U	U

Checklists of Reptiles and Amphibians

More than 50 species of reptiles, including 26 species of snakes and 16 species of turtles, have been found in Everglades National Park. The reptiles include, of course, the alligator, which is the symbol of the Everglades. Less conspicuous than the reptiles are the 18 species of amphibians that live here. Many are nocturnal. These lists represent species found within the park or nearby. Species considered exotic to Everglades National Park are marked with an asterisk (*).

Reptiles

American crocodile   *Crocodylus acutus*
American alligator   *Alligator mississippiensis*
Florida snapping turtle   *Chelydra serpentina*
Striped mud turtle   *Kinosternum bauri*
Stinkpot   *Sternotherus odoratus*
Florida box turtle   *Terrapene carolina*
Diamondback terrapin   *Malaclemys terrapin*
Peninsula cooter   *Chrysemys floridanis*
Florida redbelly turtle   *Chrysemys nelsoni*
Florida chicken turtle   *Deirochelys reticularia*
Gopher tortoise   *Gopherus polyphemus*
Atlantic green turtle   *Chelonia mydas*
Atlantic hawksbill   *Eretmochelys imbricata*
Atlantic loggerhead   *Caretta caretta*
Atlantic ridley   *Lepidochelys kempi*
Florida softshell   *Trionyx ferox*
Indopacific gecko   *Hemidactylus garnoti**
Florida reef gecko   *Shpaerodactylus notatus*
Green anole   *Anolis carolinensis*
Brown anole   *Anolis sagrai**
Knight anole   *Anolis equestris**
Common iguana   *Iguana iguana**
Ground skink   *Scincella lateralis*
Eastern glass lizard   *Ophisaurus ventralis*
Island glass lizard   *Ophisaurus compressus*
Florida green water snake   *Nerodia cyclopion*
Brown water snake   *Nerodia taxispilota*
Florida water snake   *Nerodia fasciata pictiventris*
Mangrove saltmarsh snake   *Nerodia fasciata compressicauda*
South Florida swamp snake   *Seminatrix pygaea*
Florida brown snake   *Stoeria dekayi*
Eastern garter snake   *Thamnophis sirtalis*
Peninsula ribbon snake   *Thamnophis sauritus*
Striped crayfish snake   *Regina alleni*
Eastern hognose snake   *Heterodon platyrhinos*
Southern ringneck snake   *Diadopis punctatus*
Eastern mud snake   *Farancia abacura*
Everglades racer   *Coluber constrictor*
Eastern coachwhip   *Masticophis flagellum*

Rough green snake   *Opheodrys aestivus*
Eastern indigo   *Drymarchon corais*
Corn snake   *Elaphe guttata*
Everglades rat snake   *Elaphe obsoleta*
Yellow rat snake   *Elaphe obsoleta quadrivitatta*
Florida kingsnake   *Lampropeltis getulus*
Scarlet kingsnake   *Lampropeltis triangulum*
Florida scarlet snake   *Cemophora coccinea*
Eastern coral snake   *Micrurus fulvius*
Florida cottonmouth   *Agkistrodon piscivorus*
Dusky pygmy rattlesnake   *Sistrurus miliarius*
Eastern diamondback   *Crotalus adamanteus*

Amphibians
Two-toed amphiuma   *Amphiuma means*
Greater siren   *Siren lacertina*
Everglades dwarf siren   *Pseudobranchus striatus belli*
Peninsula newt   *Notophthalmus viridescens*
Eastern spadefoot toad   *Scaphiophus holbrooki*
Greenhouse frog   *Eleuthrodactylus planirostris**
Southern toad   *Bufo terrestris*
Oak toad   *Bufo quercicus*
Florida cricket frog   *Acris gryllus*
Green treefrog   *Hyla cinerea*
Squirrel treefrog   *Hyla squirella*
Cuban treefrog   *Osteopilus septentrionalis**
Little grass frog   *Limneaodus ocularis*
Florida chorus frog   *Pseudacris nigrita*
Eastern narrow-mouth toad   *Gastrophyne carolinesis*
Pig frog   *Rana grylio*
Southern leopard frog   *Rana spenocephala*

Checklist of Trees and Tree-like Plants

A tree is defined here as a woody plant at least 12 feet high with a single trunk 2 inches or more in diameter at breast height. A tree-like plant is one with the general shape and size of a tree, but one which is not woody or otherwise fails to meet the definition. The arrangement of families generally follows Long and Lakela's *A Flora of Tropical Florida* (1971). Genera and species are listed alphabetically in each family. Nomenclature follows Avery and Loope, *Plants of Everglades National Park: A Preliminary Checklist of Vascular Plants* (1983). In the checklist, the introduced exotic species are followed by a category (key below), that describes the plants' status in the Everglades. Native plants list only their name. These categories were developed by the Florida Exotic Pest Plant Council.

Category I   Species that are invading and disrupting native plant communities in Florida.

Category II   Species that have shown a potential to invade and disrupt native plant communities.

Category III   Species persisting from cultivation or land-scape plantings and have not naturalized in the park.

PINE FAMILY: *PINACEAE*
South Florida Slash Pine   *Pinus elliotti var. densa*

BALD CYPRESS FAMILY: *TAXODIACEAE*
Pond cypress   *Taxodium ascendens*
Bald cypress   *Taxodijm distichum*

PALM FAMILY: *ARECACEAE*
Paurotis palm   *Acoelorraphe wrightii*
Silver palm   *Coccothrinax argentata*
Coconut   *Cocos nucifera* III
Royal palm   *Roystonea elata*
Cabbage palm   *Sabal palmetto*
Saw palmetto   *Serenoa repens*
Thatch palm   *Thrinax radiata*

CENTURY PLANT FAMILY: *AGAVACEAE*
False sisal   *Agave decipiens*
Sisal   *Agave sisalana* I
Spanish dagger   *Yucca aloifolia*

BANANA FAMILY: *MUSACEAE*
Banana   *Musa x paradisiaca* III

BEEFWOOD FAMILY: *CASUARINACEAE*
Australian-pine   *Casuarina equisetifolia* I
Suckering australian-pine   *Casuarina glauca* I

WILLOW FAMILY: *SALICACEAE*
Willow   *Salix caroliniana*

BAYBERRY FAMILY: *MYRICACEAE*
Wax-myrtle   *Myrica cerifera*

OAK FAMILY: *FAGACEAE*
Laurel oak   *Quercus laurifolia*
Live oak   *Quercus virginiana*

ELM FAMILY: *ULMACEAE*
Hackberry   *Celtis laevigata*
West Indian trema   *Trema lamarckianum*
Florida trema   *Trema micranthum*

MULBERRY FAMILY: *MORACEAE*
Strangler fig   *Ficus aurea*
Shortleaf fig   *Ficus citrifolia*
Red mulberry   *Morus rubra*

XIMENIA FAMILY: *OLACACEAE*
Graytwig   *Schoepfia chrysophylloides*
Tallowwood   *Ximenia americana*

BUCKWHEAT FAMILY: *POLYGONACEAE*
Pigeon plum   *Coccoloba diversifolia*
Sea grape   *Coccoloba uvifera*

FOUR-O-CLOCK FAMILY: *NYCTAGINACEAE*
Blolly   *Guapira discolor*
Pull-and-hold-back   *Pisonia aculeata*

MAGNOLIA FAMILY: *MAGNOLIACEAE*
Sweet bay   *Magnolia virginiana*

CUSTARD-APPLE FAMILY: *ANNONACEAE*
Pond apple   *Annona glabra*

LAUREL FAMILY: *LAURACEAE*
Lancewood   *Nectandra coriacea*
Red-bay   *Persea borbonia*
Avocado   *Persea americana* III

CAPER FAMILY: *CAPPARACEAE*
Jamaica caper   *Capparis cynophallophora*
Limber caper   *Capparis flexuosa*

99   ROSE FAMILY: *ROSACEAE*

West Indian cherry   *Prunus myrtifolia*

COCO-PLUM FAMILY: *CHRYSOBALANACEAE*
Coco-plum   *Chrysobalanus icaco*

PEA FAMILY: *FABACEAE*
Sweet acacia   *Acacia farnesiana*
Pineland acacia   *Acacia pinetorum*
Shy leaf   *Aeschynomene americana var. americana*
Everglades shy leaf   *Aeschynomene pratensis
                        var. pratensis*
Woman's tongue   *Albizia lebbeck* II
Orchid tree   *Bauhinia purpurea* II
            Chamaecrista aspera
Bahama senna   *Senna mexicana var. chapmanii*
            Chamaecrista deeringiana
Golden shower   *Cassia fistula* III
            Senna ligustrina
Sickle-pod   *Senna obtusifolia*
            Dalbergia brownei
Royal ponciana   *Delonix regia* III
Coral-bean   *Erythrina herbacea*
Jumbie bean   *Leucaena leucocephala* II
Wild tamarind   *Lysiloma latisiliquum*
Jamaica dogwood   *Piscidia piscipula*
Black-bead   *Pithecellobium quadalupense*
Cat's claw   *Pithecellobium unguis-cati*
Necklace pod   *Sophora tomentosa*

RUE FAMILY: *RUTACEAE*
Sour orange,lime   *Citrus spp.* III

AILANTHUS FAMILY: *SIMAROUBACEAE*
Mexican alvaradoa   *Alvaradoa amorphoides*
Paradise-tree   *Simarouba glauca*

BAY CEDAR FAMILY: *SURIANACEAE*
Bay cedar   *Suriana maritima*

BURSERA FAMILY: *BURSERACEAE*
Gumbo-limbo   *Bursera simaruba*

MAHOGANY FAMILY: *MELIACEAE*
West Indian mahogany   *Swietenia mahagoni*

MALPIGHIA FAMILY: *MALPIGHIACEAE*
Locust-berry   *Brysonima lucīda*

SPURGE FAMILY: *EUPHORBIACEAE*
Crabwood   *Gymnanthes lucida*
Bishopwood   *Bischofia javanica* I
Milk Bark   *Drypetes diversifolia*

Guiana-plum *Drypetes lateriflora*
Manchineel *Hippomane mancinella*

CASHEW FAMILY: *ANACARDIACEAE*
Poisonwood *Metopium toxiferum*
Southern sumac *Rhus copallina var. leucantha*
Brazillian-pepper *Schinus terebinthifolius* I
Hogplum *Spondias purpurea* III

HOLLY FAMILY: *AQUIFOLIACEAE*
Dahoon *Ilex cassine*
Tawnberry holly *Ilex krugiana*

BITTERSWEET FAMILY: *CELASTRACEAE*
Ground holly *Crossopetalum ilicifolium*
Rhacoma *Crossopetalum rhacoma*
Guttapercha mayten *Maytenus phyllanthoides*

MAPLE FAMILY: *ACERACEAE*
Red maple *Acer rubum*

SOAPBERRY FAMILY: *SAPINDACEAE*
Varnish-leaf *Dodonaea viscosa*
Inkwood *Exothea paniculata*
White ironwood *Hypelate trifoliata*
Spanish lime *Melicoccus bijugatus* III
Soapberry *Sapindus saponaria*

BUCKTHORN FAMILY: *RHAMNACEAE*
Coffee colubrina *Colubrina arborescens*
Lather leaf *Colubrina asiatica* I
Cuban colubrina *Colubrina cubensis*
Black ironwood *Krugiodendron ferreum*

ELAEOCARPUS FAMILY: *ELAEOCARPACEAE*
Strawberry-tree *Muntingia calabura* III

MALLOW FAMILY: *MALVACEAE*
Wild cotton *Gossypium hirsutum*
China rose *Hibiscus rosa-sinensis* III
Turk's cap *Malvaviscus arboreus var. mexicanus* III
Seaside Mahoe *Thespesia populnea* I

CANELLA FAMILY: *CANELLACEAE*
Wild-cinnamon *Canella winterana*

PAPAYA FAMILY: *CARICACEAE*
Papaya *Carica papaya* III

CACTUS FAMILY: *CACTACEAE*
Prickly apple *Cereus gracillis var. simpsonii*
Dildo *Cereus pentagonus*

MANGROVE FAMILY: *RHIZOPHORACEAE*
Red mangrove   *Rhizophora mangle*

COMBRETUM FAMILY: *COMBRETACEAE*
Black olive   *Bucida buceras* III
Buttonwood   *Conocarpus erectus*
White mangrove   *Laguncularia racemosa*
Indian almond   *Terminalia catappa* II

MYRTLE FAMILY: *MYRTACEAE*
Bottlebrush   *Callistemon viminalis* III
Spicewood   *Calyptranthes pallens var. pallens*
Myrtle-of-the-river   *Calyptranthes zuzygium*
White stopper   *Eugenia axillaris*
Spanish stopper   *Eugenia foetida*
Cajeput   *Melaleuca quinquenervia* I
Simpson stopper   *Myrcianthes fragans var. simpsonii*
Guava   *Psidium guajava* I
Long-stalked stopper   *Mosiera longipes var. longipes*

MEADOW-BEAUTY FAMILY: *MELASTOMATACEAE*
Spanish leather   *Tetrazygia bicolor*

JOE-WOOD FAMILY: *THEOPHRASTACEAE*
Joe-wood   *Jacquinia keyensis*

MYRSINE FAMILY: *MYRSINACEAE*
Marlberry   *Ardisia escallonioides*
Shoebutton ardisia   *Ardisia elliptica* I
Myrsine   *Myrsine floridana*

SAPODILLA FAMILY: *SAPOTACEAE*
Saffron-plum   *Bumelia celastrina*
    Bumelia reclinata var. reclinata
Willow bustic   *Bumelia salicifolia*
Satin leaf   *Chrysophyllum oliviforme*
Wild dilly   *Manilkara bahamensis*
Mastic   *Mastichodendron foetidissimum*

EBONY FAMILY: *EBENACEAE*
Persimmon   *Diospyros virginiana*

OLIVE FAMILY: *OLEACEAE*
Wild-olive   *Forestiera segregata var. pinetorum*
Florida-privet   *Forestiera segregata var. segregata*
Pop ash   *Fraxinus caroliniana*

DOGBANE FAMILY: *APOCYNACEAE*
Lucky nut   *Thevetia peruviana* III
Pearl-berry   *Vallesia antillana*

BORAGE FAMILY: *BORAGINACEAE*

Smooth strongbark *Bourreria cassinifolia*
Strongbark *Bourreria ovata*
Geiger-tree *Cordia sebestena*

BLACK MANGROVE FAMILY: *AVICENNIACEAE*
Black mangrove *Avicennia germinans*

VERBENA FAMILY: *VERBENACEAE*
Fiddlewood *Citharexylum fruticosum*
Java glory-bowers *Clerodendrum speciosissimum* III

POTATO FAMILY: *SOLANACEAE*
Potato tree *Solanum erianthum*

MADDER FAMILY: *RUBIACEAE*
Seven-year apple *Casasia clusiifolia*
Buttonbush *Cephalanthus occidentalis*
Black torch *Erithalis fruticosa*
Velvet seed *Guettarda elliptica*
Rough velvet-seed *Guettarda scabra*
Firebush *Hamelia patens*
Indigo-berry *Randia aculeata*

HONEYSUCKLE FAMILY: *CAPRIFOLIACEAE*
Southern elderberry *Sambucus canadensis*

ASTER FAMILY: *ASTERACEAE*
Groundsel-tree *Baccharis glomeruliflora*
Saltbush *Baccharis halimifolia*

Handbook 143

The National Park Service expresses its appreciation to all those persons who made the preparation and production of this handbook possible. Special thanks are extended to Frank Craighead, Sr., Pat Miller, Bill Robertson, and Saul Schiffman, who read the manuscript and provided much useful information. The checklists were compiled over many years by various members of the Everglades National Park staff. The Service also gratefully acknowledges the financial support given this handbook project by the Everglades Natural History Association, a nonprofit group that assists interpretive efforts at the park. The cover photograph is by Glenn van Nimwegen.

National Park Service
U.S. Department of the Interior

As the Nation's principal conservation agency, the Department of the Interior has responsibility for most of our nationally owned public lands and natural resources. This includes fostering the wisest use of our land and water resources, protecting our fish and wildlife, preserving the environmental and cultural values of our national parks and historical places, and providing for the enjoyment of life through outdoor recreation. The Department assesses our energy and mineral resources and works to assure that their development is in the best interest of all our people. The Department also has a major responsibility for American Indian reservation communities and for people who live in island territories under U.S. administration.

Everglades
Wildguide